Pruning

KLAAS T. NOORDHUIS
INTRODUCTION BY RICHARD ROSENFELD

 **REBO**
PRODUCTIONS

Dedicated to Dorothea, Patron Saint of Gardeners

© 1996 Zuid Boekprodukties, Lisse
© 1996 Published by Rebo Productions Ltd
Jacket design and layout: Ton Wienbelt, The Netherlands
Photography editor: Marieke Uiterwijk, TextCase
Production: TextCase, The Netherlands
Translation: Guy Shipton for First Edition Translations Ltd, Great Britain
Typesetting: Computech for First Edition Translations Ltd, Great Britain

ISBN 1 901094 43 X

Contents

INTRODUCTION

The best job in gardening isn't creating a new one from scratch, it's finding an old walled garden, the key lost and the door jammed, that no-one has been in for years, that's coiled and barbed with weeds, with wet leaves that have turned to mud, and frogs and toads and snakes. Finding ancient trees and rhododendrons, and wisterias that have sent out branches that jut and run across ground like a runner bean .

What's required is not so much pruning as sculpting. Not the 'Do this, do that' kind of pruning', '3cm here, and don't you dare make a mistake', but the hacking and thwacking kind, slicing off big fat dead branches and making the sad look dapper. It's incredibly therapeutic.

Most shrubs, and even trees, run away with themselves, doing all the things they shouldn't. Like putting on masses of growth, and blowing up like balloons, which might suit their genetic make-up but not your typical garden. They need to be kept shipshape and orderly, not just to prevent a ridiculous degree of excess, but to impose style on the shapeless; to create surprise vistas through branches, and gaps for framing set features. The Japanese are so skilled at doing it, it's part of their gardening make-up. Isn't it time we copied them?

Take two examples. Ceanothus thyrsiflorus *is a vigorous Californian with fantastic glossy green leaves and arching branches, and dark blue flowers in spring. Though called a shrub it quickly becomes a small tree about 4.5m (15ft) high. But it also gets incredibly blobby, and looks far smarter with adventurous pruning, turning it a weeping shape. Even the dense, floppy evergreen shrub* Prunus laurocerasus *'Magnolifolia', with its scented white*

spring flowers, can be sculptured into a flowering upright. Pruning is as much as about style as health. Yet pruning sounds such a bore.

Technically, scientifically precise, and behind the flying snap of a secateur a whole library of when and how, laterals and leaders, and ways of breaking apical dominance (which basically means if you cut off the top of a stem, new shoots start appearing below). But don't get twitchy. Pruning is jolly god fun, you just need the tips from the experts. Books like this make the key difference between getting it right, making a botch, and having to wait a year before your clematis flowers. Books like this save time.

Part of the art of gardening is also knowing when to be, and not to be cavalier. It's obvious pelargoniums get pruned in the growing season, when you can plant up the prunings as cuttings, giving you even more plants. But if you can't manage it then, why not in winter? I know it counters received wisdom, and you won't have a brilliant success rate, but it can be done. Pruning fruit trees is a totally different matter. You've got to know when to take liberties.

The funny thing about gardening is that it starts as a huge artistic enterprise, slashing down old growth, then planting pinks and blues and greens, ordering your cast of plants about, but it always ends up with detail. In the greenhouse, hunched over seed trays, followed by stints in the border, nose to bark with the plants, snapping off dead twigs. All gardening, like it or not, ends with pruning. It's like fine tuning a vintage Bentley. Master the art, and everything looks a thousand times better.

Richard Rosenfeld, East Sussex, 1996

Conditions for healthy growth

Pruning is necessary for many reasons. Not only does it stimulate the production of flowers and fruit but it also keeps a plant in good shape and growing healthily.

Guidance for young trees

Here, the lowest branches have been removed too late. The large wounds will be visible for a long time afterwards.

When planting young trees, we like to imagine just how they will look when fully grown. It's a shame that many trees never reach that stage for a whole variety of reasons. Whether through disease or being planted in the wrong position, a tree's failure is usually attributable to ignorance on the part of the gardener.

A young tree should be pruned back gradually. If a tree has two rival leaders, one of these branches must be removed annually so that the tree will eventually have one clear central leader.

A young tree needs the support of a stake, otherwise its trunk will shift about in the ground, tearing off its rootlets. A stake should always be placed on the windward side of the tree, which prevents the tree from being battered against the pole when the wind blows. A stake should be secured to a tree using a tree collar, although this can often cause new problems.

All too often people forget to remove tree collars after two or three years, when a trunk's diameter will have increased. The consequence is that the trunk becomes pinched at that point, and a strong wind can snap the trunk in two where the tree collar once fixed it to the stake. For this reason, it is vital that you check the collar regularly during the tree's growing season. If the main stem is still too flimsy to remove the stake, then the collar should be of an ample girth to allow for the tree's future growth.

Stakes prevent wind-rock, which can damage young rootlets and hence diminish the uptake of water.

6

Protecting trees

Should you be performing any building work in the vicinity, to prevent damage to the tree's phloem the tree should be protected somehow, and rubble should not be dumped at the base of the trunk. Fortunately, it is common practice amongst builders for tree bark to be protected by vertical planking before work commences.

Most damage to trees is caused by cars. Concrete bollards and tree-tubs can provide a solution to direct damage, but soil compaction from cars driving over unpaved areas can also be prevented. The ground driven over is subject to less pressure if large paving stones are laid over it. Gas leaks also cost the lives of many trees. The oxygen in the soil becomes replaced by gas and, as a result, the roots asphyxiate. Do not hesitate to call the gas company if you suspect a leakage. Remember, if a tree is looking unhealthy the cause is usually to be found below ground.

Trees are often used as supports for washing lines. This should not be done as the rope will grow into the tree after only a few years and will cause a great deal of permanent damage. The same is true of wire fencing, which is often fixed to trees with nails. Apart from the immediate damage to the tree, wires and nails will cause costly future problems when a chainsaw is used to cut up the tree for logs and firewood.

I was once faced with many serious problems in the garden of the house I had just moved to. As well as the pruning having fallen badly

This Acer palmatum *'Dissectum Atropur-pureum' does not require pruning. It already has a naturally perfect shape.*

This weeping beech's rootstock has begun producing suckers. These suckers are the first shoots to come into leaf.

behind, many other things were causing the trees to suffer: a parking place had been situated under an old tree; heaps of rubble had been dumped underneath other trees; a great deal of damage had been caused by goats eating the bark; an open hearth had been made in a wooded area; wire fencing had been nailed to trees; washing lines had grown into trees; and a wasps' nest in an old apple tree had been sprayed with gasoline!

Some of the trees close to the house were much too wet because the drains were blocked. This may all seem rather extreme, but I fear that the garden concerned is no great exception: take a walk through your own garden to see if it complies with all the conditions for healthy growth.

In short, the message here is that tree maintenance is more than just pruning.

Trees have been pruned wrongly for centuries, as this painting by Meindert Hobbema (1689), The Avenue at Middelharnis, bears witness. The correct proportions are one third trunk and two thirds crown.

Preventing damage by animals

In harsh winters when there is a lot of snow on the ground, animals can cause a great deal of damage to trees. Some of this damage can be easily avoided, for example, by setting out extra food for such animals as hares. Rams and goats will harm the trees in any garden, and treating the wounds made by them will not help very much. It is far better to remove the animals. An untethered goat will run to the first tree it sees and start to gnaw away at the bark whether it is hungry or not. Knowing how high goats can jump, a goat-pen is of little use.

Sheep, on the other hand, only eat tree bark once their other food source has run out. It is safe to let them wander through an orchard where there is enough grass for them to eat or when they have been given enough fodder.

The greatest sense of security is provided by wire fencing erected around trees. If rabbits are the only animals in an orchard, then young tree trunks can be enclosed with specially made plastic sheeting cut from a roll. If this is not available, a plastic waste-pipe cut in half lengthways will serve just as well.

Voles cause a great deal of damage underground. They particularly like using mole runs. If you persist in removing moles from your garden, this will simultaneously reduce any vole problem.

Preventing diseases and infections

Healthy plant growth (in which your tree maintenance plays a great part) will prevent many diseases and infections arising in the first place. Few tree diseases are directly related to pruning, and always working hygienically will deter diseases from occurring. It is important to remove all prunings and loppings from underneath trees, particularly in the case of fruit trees. Prunings left to lie around can result in the growth of all manner of diseases, (I shall return to this subject in Chapter 5, "*Pruning fruit trees*").

Coral spot (*Nectria cinnabarina*) is often found on dead wood, or under trees and shrubs. Little orange-red spots can be seen dotted all

Large wounds take a long time to heal and grow over. Rot and infections often set in as a result, so try to keep all wounds as small as possible.

over the dead twigs and branches. Coral spot can spread from dead wood to living tissue. Therefore, remove any infected branches and burn them.

Disinfect the pruning knife and cover the wound with a protective paint. Also, making small cuts will give the fungus little opportunity to gain access to the tree.

The purpose of pruning

The purposes of pruning range from encouraging the production of good flowers and fruit to maintaining the plant in good shape and health.

Reducing the size of a tree or bush because it has become too big is not pruning – this is simply cutting back. A plant that will grow into a specimen too large for its surroundings should never have been planted there in the first place.

The best remedy is to replace with one that will grow to a more suitable size for that location.

Several tree surgery techniques have gone in and out of fashion. Here, an old tree trunk has been filled with concrete. Grooves made in the concrete mimic the tree's bark.

The final size of a plant should be taken into consideration from the very outset. Shrubs come in all sizes, even within the same genera. Both lilac (*Syringa*) and mock orange (*Philadelphus*) vary in height from 60cm (24in) to 4m (13ft). There are more than enough to choose from. However, if for some reason a tree or shrub cannot be left to attain its natural mature size, it is possible to employ topiary techniques if the species concerned is suited to such treatment – which the majority of shrubs are.

Tree surgery describes (perhaps too nicely?) the prolongation of life of what are, usually, old trees. Just as we sometimes debate whether prolonging a person's life is always the right thing to do, we are just as entitled to ask ourselves the same thing in regard to trees. A tree will reach a certain point when it has come to the end of its life. Instead of spending a great deal of money trying to recuperate an old tree we should weigh up whether or not our money might not be better spent on a younger (established) tree.

Improvement of flowers and fruit yield

Many plants can be pruned to produce larger flowers or to ensure a longer flowering period. "Rubbing out" or disbudding is the removal of lateral buds from, for example, such plants as carnations, roses, and chrysanthemums so that the apical bud produces stronger growth and larger, fuller flowers.

A number of perennials (such as *Centaurea*) can be cut back immediately after flowering to make them bloom once again the same season. Phlox can have several of its flowering shoots cut back before midsummer. These pruned flower shoots will form new side-shoots, all of which will flower later. Whether a flower-bed stays in bloom all summer, therefore, depends not simply on the plants chosen but also on the way they are handled during the growing season.

Just as pruning some plants before they begin flowering ensures an

improvement in the development of their flowers, so the removal of some fruits from a heavily laden tree or shrub results in the better development of the remaining fruit. Thinning out bunches of grapes is an example of this. It is often the case, especially with trees that have just been planted, that a lot of unripe fruit is removed from the tree before the fruit reaches maturity. And particularly abundant fruit yields will mean that the branches will have to be supported to prevent them from snapping under their heavy burden.

More energy goes back into the bulb when daffodil seed-heads are picked off after flowering. This ensures even better flowers the following spring.

Maintaining shape

The idea behind pruning is to give shrubs a natural appearance. Although bushes in nature do not receive regular prunings, we can attempt to prune a garden shrub into the shape in which it would look its best if it were in its natural environment - an ideal shape rarely seen in nature. It is important to prune regularly, and regularity (i.e. annually) is even more important than the way in which it is done. The ratio of roots to branches should remain in balance. It is also unwise to prune too much all at once as this upsets the balance: powerful regenerative growth would be the result. The water shoots which subsequently appear will only mean more pruning to be done the following year.

Preventing new growth

Trees are often cut down to a stump ("stooled") in order to stimulate young, bushy growth. However, sometimes we want to prevent new

11

shoots from growing from the stump. Commercially produced chemical paints will stop shoots growing altogether. Use a brush to apply the undiluted paint on to the freshly sawn stump.

The paint is absorbed into the stump and roots, which kills them. Felled conifers do not need such treatment. With the exception of yew (*Taxus*), conifers fail to regenerate.

Simply removing the young shoots when they appear will result in the gradual weakening of the stump and, after a few years, it will die.

Retaining species type

A number of cultivars degenerate or mutate in their growth patterns. The golden elm (*Ulmus carpinifolia* 'Wredei'), for example, can suddenly start to produce quick-growing green branches.

Nature does not always agree with humanity's attempts to produce cultivated varieties, and tries to revert to the species' natural growth pattern. Suckers will need pruning out in order to maintain the cultivar's appearance. These suckers should be removed as close to their source as possible as they often spring from the rootstock.

Recovery after transplantation

A plant needs its root system to supply its upper parts with water and food. As we have already seen, there is a balance between the amount of plant material above and below ground.

Many roots are broken off during transplantation, which disturbs this balance. The few roots left intact will fail to provide an adequate water

A constrictive tree collar should be removed before it is too late.

supply. As a result, leaves will hang limply or, in the worst instance, dry out altogether. It is unlikely that all the roots will be saved during transplantation, even if it appears that they have been.

The majority of the imperceptible root-hairs will have been lost. As a consequence, drastic pruning back of the upper tree may be necessary to bring it into balance with the roots. Thin out branches if this is the case rather than pruning them hard back (thinning out will also have a less devastating impact on the tree's appearance than cutting hard back).

Roots which are too long for the hole dug for a the tree should not be bent to make them fit. Shorten the woody roots instead. As far as possible, try not to harm the root-hairs. Tall or standard trees should always be provided with a stake for support. This will prevent the newly formed root-hairs from being damaged and hence endangering the tree's water supply.

The is a serious risk that a tree could die if its roots have been badly damaged whilst digging.

The only course of action is a radical "candelabra" pruning to bring the remaining roots and foliage into balance. This trimming involves sawing back all the branches close to the trunk, leaving the lower branches longer than the upper ones.

After being sawn down, the stumps should be treated with a suitable chemical paint if regenerative growth is to be stemmed.

The lower branches should be sawn back to about 1m (3ft) and the upper ones to about 50cm (20in). Leave the central leader intact.

The tree will grow back from adventitious or dormant buds. This trimming not only restores the balance between roots and foliage but also reduces considerably the risk of the newly planted tree being blown over.

Recovery of neglected plants

The best course of action for most shrubs that have been neglected for several years is to stool them to encourage the production of large quantities of new shoots.

Twigs formed on these new shoots should be well thinned out the following year. This will give the remaining ones more light and hence make them stronger.

Shrubs which flower on current growth will flower the same year they are pruned. However, shrubs which flower on last season's wood cannot be expected to bloom the first year after pruning.

Whether to do the pruning yourself or have it done professionally?

Root pruning may be necessary during transplantation.

Before you start pruning, you should ask yourself whether the best plan is to do it yourself or to call in a professional. This book aims to equip you will all the knowledge necessary to do the pruning yourself, but in some cases you may be more tempted to hire a professional.

Having someone do your pruning and remove the clippings is costly: more time is spent cutting up the loppings and taking them away than in actual pruning! However, you can always compromise. Ask a professional to do only the technical pruning work while you deal with the cutting up and disposal of any waste material. This will save you from having to invest in specialized pruning tools and the task will be completed more quickly.

Even in medium-sized gardens, an experienced gardener will accomplish the annual pruning in one morning.

However, you will have to be prepared for a professional to come in on separate occasions to deal with, say, a vine which needs pruning earlier in the year.

Professionals work faster than amateurs because they always have the correct tools with them. And good gardeners will have brought along a shredder for cutting up wood waste. Clippings and loppings can thus be tidied up more quickly, and the organic material produced can be used to the benefit of your garden.

Next page: suckers being removed from a corkscrew hazel (Corylus avellana 'Contorta').

Pruning times and tools

This chapter considers the time of year when pruning should occur, the tools required for pruning, and what to do with waste material.

When should you prune?

Not all plants can be pruned at just any time of the year. Even so, no matter what the season, there is always something which requires pruning. Frost-sensitive shrubs and roses can be pruned in spring; several kinds of perennials can be partially pruned before midsummer so that they produce a better display of flowers; fruit trees can be pruned in summer; and autumn and winter are good times for pruning trees and shrubs.

A shrub's branch structure is easier to see in winter. The removal of inner branches then becomes simpler.

Summer pruning

Pruning in summer is difficult because foliage makes it hard to see the branches. Summer pruning mainly involves removing branches that overhang paths or those which could become dangerous. The advantage of summer pruning is that wounds heal faster, thus preventing diseases from infecting trees and shrubs. Summer pruning is also recommended for several species to encourage improved fruit yield. The more light given to a red or white currant, the better the development of its fruit bunches. A few leaves are removed from tomato plants for the same reason. Long, new shoots on small apple and pear trees can be pruned back once the leader bud has formed.

Winter pruning

As a rule, winter is the time for hard pruning, the reason simply being that this is the time of year when gardeners have more time to spare. The big advantage of winter pruning is that branches are more easily seen. A leafless branch is also more easily dispatched than one in full

leaf. Trees and shrubs can be pruned when they are dormant. Remember that sap starts to rise early in many plants. Make sure you prune back birches, maples, and vines before March. The majority of plants can be pruned without problems until April.

By pruning in winter you will avoid damaging any herbaceous undergrowth around the trees. It is therefore recommended that pruning begin early, preferably at the beginning of November, should any bulbs have been planted beneath the trees and shrubs concerned.

It is better not to prune during severe frosts, as frozen branches can easily split. Not only is this dangerous to the person doing the pruning but it also results in unnecessary damage to the tree.

If you must prune rhododendrons, then it is better not to do it in sunny weather.

Problem plants Extremely frost-sensitive plants should be dealt with only when the likelihood of frost has passed. It is best to prune such plants after mid-April. Rose stems almost always freeze which results in the whole plant becoming frost-bitten if it has been pruned back low in the autumn.

Some plants, such as vines, maples, kiwis, and walnut, will "bleed" severely if pruned in April: sap already rising in these plants will pour out of any fresh wounds. These plants should not be pruned after February as this stream of sap is almost impossible to stem. Pruning can only begin again from July onwards.

Some plants, such as box (*Buxus sempervirens*), rhododendron,

17

beech (*Fagus*), and hornbeam (*Carpinus*), will not tolerate direct sunshine on their bark as this quickly leads to scorching. Therefore, do not prune these plants in sunny weather. To prevent scorching, these plants can be temporarily covered with white cloth or sheets in case the sun suddenly comes out. This will allow light, air, and moisture to pass through, but filters the light.

Young trees sensitive to scorching include ash (*Fraxinus*), maple (*Acer*), lime (*Tilia*), and plane (*Platanus*).

Woodchips can be spread underneath shrubs or used to "reinforce" a wooded path.

Dealing with waste material

Don't just throw all your pruned and lopped branches on to a heap: this only creates more work later (carrying them away or cutting them up). Always saw larger branches where they branch off from the parent stem. This will make them easier to stack up. Lay the branches in the same direction, not criss-crossed over each other. This makes the it easier to pick up the stack later.

Light-weight branches and twigs can be composted if your compost heap can be left for a few years. Heavier branches are best stacked into a woodpile, creating a retreat for hedgehogs and other wildlife.

A shredder should be used when there are simply too many branches to deal with all at once.

Shredders can either spit out woodchips on to a heap or else spread them around the garden. Never allow woodchips to become heaped up in between shrubs: such heaps are an ideal growing place for fungi.

Amongst other things, woodchips, compost, and fallen leaves help protect bulbs underground. So never throw away any valuable organic material!

Woodchips should be spread evenly around shrubs or over paths. However, the disadvantage of doing this is that you will no longer be able to hoe the soil.

Any weeds that grow through the chips will have to be removed by hand or sprayed with a weedkiller.

Tree trunks can be used in gardens for edging paths and borders as well as for firewood. Needle-covered branches from conifers can be used as a protective cover for frost-sensitive perennials.

Twigs can be used like willow switches to support the flowers of perennials which have become top-heavy. Sawn-off branches can be laid on the ground in snowy winters to minimize the damage to living wood caused by rabbits and hares. Finally, you can always have your waste wood taken away!

Right-handed secateurs are awkward when held in the left hand. The secateurs will be difficult to handle, and the pruning done will harm the shrub.

Pruning tools   The great majority of pruning operations can be carried out using the following:

- gardening gloves
- a pair of secateurs
- a long-handled lopper
- a pruning saw
- a bow saw (a small model with a handguard)

Some of the pruning tools required for a medium-sized garden: secateurs, a pruning saw for larger branches, a fold-away pocket saw, a bow saw, and a Grecian (curved) saw.

Only four tools are needed for winter pruning in small gardens: a pair of secateurs (left or right-handed), a long-handled lopper, a pruning saw with pistol-grip, and a small bow saw.

Hand shears are best for topiary work, and hedging shears are indispensable for clipping hedges. Pruning knives are employed a great deal in nurseries but are not recommended for the inexperienced.

People are all too often tempted to start using electrical tools. These are often completely unnecessary, never mind the frightful din they make. A good pair of shears can cut back a hedge just as quickly and neatly as electric hedge-trimmers. The result is much more attractive when performed by hand, especially with such hedges as box (*Buxus sempervirens*). Only if your garden is very large should you consider purchasing a large bow saw, a pole pruner with a telescopic pole, and, if absolutely necessary, a small chainsaw. Trees in forestry plantations are often stooled with tree mowers. I cannot stress enough that a machine like this should only be used by a professional.

All these gardening tools must be keen-edged, and must be oiled after use to keep them that way. Spare blades can be bought to replace blunted ones for the more expensive tools. Bow-saw blades are not expensive, and so can be replaced regularly. It is better not to use saws

A good pair of secateurs is an investment for life.

with plastic handles. Since most pruning takes place in cold weather, plastic handles could become brittle and so break off. However, it is a good idea to choose tools which are brightly coloured as these will be easier to see when laid down somewhere in the garden during a moment of distraction.

Pruning tends to make the garden look rather disorderly at first, making tools easier to loose.

Electric hedge-trimmers are not suited to all kinds of hedging. Consequently, hand shears should still form a part of your basic equipment.

Hedging shears   Shears are essential for clipping hedges. They can also be used to maintain lawn edging. Hand shears are for more detailed work, being a smaller version of hedging shears.

Check to see whether the shears have buffers before buying them. It does not make much difference whether a pair of shears has straight or waved blades as long as they are sharp.

Electric hedge-trimmers can sometimes be awkward to use.

Long-handled loppers   Where spiny branches and stems need cutting, it is nice to be able to prune these without having to hold on to them. Long-handled loppers are ideal for cutting rose stems.

Pruning knives   Pruning knives are often used in nurseries as they are very useful for cutting out buds and young lateral shoots. However, secateurs are better for ordinary garden use, not least because their bright red

handles make them easier to find again when carelessly put down somewhere.

Large bow saws   A large bow saw is used not so much for pruning but for cutting up loppings and toppings so that these can be piled up neatly into heaps or made into firewood.
People are all too quick to start using a chainsaw. In most cases, an ordinary bow saw will do the job just as well.
Always ensure that the blade is keen.
What is more, your neighbours will be very grateful that you have taken them into consideration as far as noise is concerned!

Most branches can be sawn off using a bow saw, which makes a chainsaw quite unnecessary in a medium-sized garden.

Telescopic poles   Telescopic poles are useful when cutting or sawing off high branches. A lopper with a drawstring or a pruning saw can be mounted on to the telescopic pole, allowing much pruning work to be carried out from the ground.

Most branches can be sawn off using a bow saw, which makes a chainsaw quite unnecessary in a medium-sized garden.

Pruning and safety   Many accidents could occur during pruning. One little slip can result in serious injury, seeing as how the tools required always need to be sharp. This is why gardening gloves should always be worn. Most

People are too easily tempted to rush for the chainsaw. This shrub can be trimmed more neatly and just as quickly using long-handled loppers or even a small tree saw.

pruning needs to be done in the winter. Bark will be wet and slippery from algal growth, making it easy for a saw to slip. Therefore, always think first before taking any action.

Harm to your eyes can be avoided by wearing protective goggles. You should see a doctor immediately should any injury occur. It is also far from an unnecessary luxury to have a first-aid box at the ready whenever pruning work is being carried out.

Using a ladder

It is not at all easy to put a ladder up against a tree. A ladder should always be placed against a tree at an angle of 70 degrees. This is the safest position.

Do not pull an extendible ladder out too far; there should be a sufficient overlap of both sections. A ladder should reach to at least 1m (3ft) above the spot where you are to work. Wear shoes with ridged soles and keep both feet on the rungs at all times. Never stand with one foot on the ladder and the other on a branch. Never allow more than one person to stand on the ladder. Reposition the ladder frequently, as leaning over can be dangerous.

Keep the ladder secured with rope whenever possible. Do not use a ladder in a strong wind.

Using a chainsaw

Many accidents occur with chainsaws. If you really have to use one then you must stick to the following rules:

Consider possible noise pollution when using a chainsaw. A lot of work can be accomplished silently using a keen-edged bow saw.

A helmet, earmuffs, protective trousers, and steel-capped boots are all necessary when working with a chainsaw.

- Do not let anyone under the age of 18 use a chainsaw.
- Make sure that there is always someone within earshot.
- Wear protective clothing, including protective shoes.
- Only use a chainsaw at ground level and not on a ladder or in a tree; always hold the chainsaw firmly with both hands.
- Do not use a chainsaw when there is no wind or in foggy weather.
- Chainsaws emit a harmful exhaust.
- Only handle the chainsaw's workings once its motor has been turned off.
- Allow nobody within a radius of several metres whilst work is in progress. Keep children out of the area! The chainsaw should never be pointed directly towards someone.
- A well greased chain makes a chainsaw safer.

Using a shredder

Protective clothing is essential when using a shredder. Always wear gardening gloves and safety goggles. Zipped-up jackets with close-fitting sleeves should be worn: loose clothing can be caught up in the machine.

Since branches and twigs can be pulled to one side, you should wear a visor to protect your face and a helmet to protect your head.

Keep your hands at a safe distance from the machine. Whatever happens, make sure that your hands never enter the feeder tray.

Never give animals toppings to eat from a perennial border. There is a big risk that they will contain poisonous plants, or parts thereof. (Karl Föster's perennial garden in Potsdam.)

Pruning for beginners

This chapter is for those who are neither gardening enthusiasts nor prepared to wrestle through half a book before being able to cut off their first branch.

The guidelines in this chapter do not comply entirely with strict gardening rules, but to do nothing at all would be much worse than ignoring them!

Topiary may look difficult, but of all pruning activities it is in fact the easiest.

A general list of rules

A few pruning rules follow which apply to all situations:

- Pruning is not the same as trimming back.
- Hedging shears and a carpenter's saw are not pruning devices.
- It is better to prune and get it wrong than not to prune at all.
- It is better to prune a bush with the result that it has fewer flowers than to neglect it (which results in fewer flowers anyway).
- Pruning is mostly courage, only partly knowledge.
- Do not worry about flowers: even when a bush is pruned back one third there is no significant decrease in the quantity of flowers.
- Remember that these rules do not apply to the butterfly bush (*Buddleia*), the ornamental almond (*Prunus triloba*), and the grapevine (*Vitis*).
- Never cut conifers back to bare wood (except yew): a gap will remain a gap!
- Prune back all shrubs in spring (March-April).
- It is quite all right to prune back shrubs when in flower.
- *Topping* trees is fundamentally wrong.
- Prune after leaves have fallen from the branches: the branching structure can then be seen more easily.
- If you are left-handed you will be unable to prune with right-handed secateurs. Buy a left-handed pair!

Concerning all trees and shrubs:

- you should first cut away all dead wood;
- cut off broken branches or laterals at their base;
- cut off a branch where it crosses or rubs against another; and
- remove branches which hang awkwardly or dangerously over paths.

Simple basic principles for different types of plant

This section deals with the basic principles for pruning trees, shrubs, conifers, hedging, roses, climbers, fruit trees, soft fruit, and perennials.

Trees

Topping You may feel that a tree is getting too big for a particular part of your garden. Even so, you should not top it. If a tree is topped it will lose its shape permanently. Young trees are sometimes topped once they reach a height of 3m (10ft) so that they produce a broad crown. Plane trees (*Platanus*) respond well to this treatment.

Pruning up If a tree has become too tall it can be pruned or crowned up. All branches from up to one third of the trunk can be removed. Always leave two thirds of the crown standing so that you do not disturb the tree's balance too much.

"Candelabra" pruning This is the last resort for saving a tree. It involves cutting back all the tree's branches to leave just stumps. The

Clipped spheres top hawthorn standards. Shaping spheres is an option for anyone who is afraid of pruning. Little experience is needed, only a great deal of patience. (The garden of A. van Wieringen.)

lower branches are left with longer stumps than the upper branches. You must bear in mind that the tree's natural shape will never return once you take this course of action.

Pollarding Some trees, such as willow, poplar, and lime are well suited to pollarding. Pollarding involves sawing off the trunk at a height of about 2-3m (6-10ft). At least once every five years prune back all shoots which have grown from this point.

Felling It may be necessary to fell a tree to protect a building. It's a pity that this should have to happen. The tree should never have been planted there in the first place. A lesson can be learned from this: always consider the tree's final height before planting it so that felling will not become necessary. Plant trees where they can be left in peace for 100 years or more.

And cut back laterals on young trees when they grow above the tree's apex.

Pruning Trees are best pruned when no longer in leaf as their branch structure is then easily seen. Try to remember how the tree looked in summer and how far down the branches bent owing to the weight of their leaves.

Remember that the only exceptions regarding pruning times are the maple (*Acer*), walnut (*Juglans*), birch (*Betula*), and chestnut (*Aesculus*). To prevent bleeding, prune these trees before January or in the summer from June onwards.

Clipped spheres top hawthorn standards. Shaping spheres is an option for anyone who is afraid of pruning. Little experience is needed, only a great deal of patience. (The garden of A. van Wieringen.)

If trees are crowned up in time, then the wounds made will be fairly small. This pruning provides sufficient light for groundcover plants to grow beneath the tree.

Shrubs As I pointed out earlier, pruning shrubs entails something other than just trimming back. To prune is to thin out. This thinning out, which involves the complete removal of whole branches, should be carried out evenly throughout the whole bush. People are often tempted to prune only the outermost branches because these are the easiest to get at. The inner branches will not be at all difficult to reach if a pruning saw and long-handled lopper are used. Sometimes only the partial pruning of a branch is required, making its complete removal unnecessary. Cut off the branch at its point of origin, and also remove inward-growing branches. If you do this you will not be able to tell where branches have been removed. Once again, I should like to emphasize that four kinds of pruning tools should always be to hand when pruning shrubs as they need to be used interchangeably: secateurs, a long-handled lopper, a pruning saw, and a small bow saw.

Conifers Charming dwarf conifers often grow into giants. Therefore, begin to remove the outermost growth tips early in early spring or in summer. Do not cut the apex. Removing a growth tip is known professionally as "stopping." Stopping promotes the development of bushier, denser, and thus more attractive conifers. I hope all this does away with the notion that conifers require no attention!

Conifers also need trimming several times each year when they are

In order to rejuvenate a bush, cut back only its thickest branches to just above ground level. The bush will rejuvenate completely after three years if a third of its branches is removed annually.

used for hedging. It is necessary to trim them *little* and *often* – it is impossible to make hedges smaller once they have been allowed to grow too wide. If, because of neglect, your hedge has become too wide, uprooting it and planting a new hedge is (sadly) the only option available.

Cutting through the foliage of large-leafed, evergreen shrubs, such as this cherry laurel (Prunus laurocerasus 'Caucasica'), is unattractive: it is better to use secateurs rather than hedging shears.

Hedging plants When clipping a hedge, look ahead of you along the length of the hedge and not at your snipping shears. Stretch a length of string along young hedges before they are clipped and use a spirit level to make sure this is straight. Many people, even those who often clip hedges, are tempted to cut deeply into the base. Do not do this. If anything, the base should be left somewhat wider to let more light reach the lower branches and so create a bushier hedge.

A hedge should be clipped at least twice a year. There is no maximum number of clipping sessions, so clip a hedge as often as you like. Beech (*Fagus sylvatica*) and box (*Buxus sempervirens*) are the exceptions to this rule (see Chapter 10, *"Pruning according to plant genus"*).

Roses What happens to roses if they are not pruned? The bush becomes overgrown with branches which prevent light from entering, and the lower part of the bush becomes bare. Remember that almost all roses are budded on rootstock, and so they are not natural plants.

The lateral shoots of a climbing rose can be pruned back annually once the rose has reached maturity.

Cultivated roses need to be maintained by pruning. Roses are classified into several groups, each of which requires a different style of pruning. Below are some general pruning tips according to rose group: *Hybrid teas* (normal bush roses up to 1.2m (4ft) in height): cut back all stems to 30cm (12in) above ground level (40cm/16in if necessary). *Shrub roses* (larger bush roses): thin out the bushes, but do not shorten the stems. *Climbing roses* (trained roses): shorten protruding laterals and tie in younger shoots jutting out to the front, or else remove them. Never cut back a climber to the ground as it will take a year to come into bloom again. *Standard roses* (roses which have been grafted on short or tall stock): prune standard roses as you would hybrid teas. Thin out weeping standards a little, but do not prune them back. *Modern miniature roses*: thin them out, prune them back or cut them down to ground level – you can do what you like with them! Suckers growing from the rootstock are common in all grafted roses, and these must be removed as close to their origin as possible. The differences between these rootstock shoots and those from the cultivated rose scion are always easy to spot in terms of leaf or stem colour, the number of leaves, and the stem's speed of growth.

Climbers

It is more important to position climbers up against a wall or to bind them to a trellis or a drainpipe than it is to prune them. Moreover, pruning them is much easier when they have been well fastened. The central leader of a well trained climber can be seen clearly and is not be so easily cut off by mistake. The protruding laterals in need of pruning are also more obvious to the eye when the central leader is clearly visible. The central leader will not be so obvious in neglected climbers that have grown into tangled knots, with laterals sticking out all over the place. It will be impossible to know where to begin. Therefore, neglected climbers should be cut down or sawn off at their base - and promise yourself afterwards to care for any climbers you plant in future from the very outset. This will involve training them well first, and then pruning them back regularly. Winter pruning is recommended as the leader stem can then be found easily.

Fruit trees

A fruit tree produces two kinds of shoot (buds): *growth shoots* and *fruiting spurs*. Fruiting spurs are only a few centimetres long. In comparison, growth shoots can sometimes grow up to 50cm (20in) in length. Fruiting spurs produce blossom and then fruit in the spring, and, consequently, should be pruned as little as possible. Shoots produced by growth buds can be pruned back hard. Do not forget that the bud below an incision always grows outwards again: you should consider in advance which direction you want any new branches to grow. Prune a shoot just above those buds you consider to be pointing in the right direction. By doing this you will be influencing the tree's future growth pattern through pruning. Even professionals take a moment to consider each bud before pruning.

The training of climbers should begin as soon as they have been purchased. On your return home, remove the supporting cane and label from the plant immediately to prevent it from being choked by these at a later stage.

Right: from the very start, hedging conifers need to be pruned back twice each summer. This photograph shows a four-year old Thuja occidentalis *'Brabant.'*

Soft fruit

The stems of blackberries and raspberries which have borne fruit should be cut back to ground level at the end of summer or in early spring. Young stems which will bear fruit the following summer can be tied in again. Currants and gooseberries can be pruned in the same way as shrubs. First remove the dead wood, then any stems which rub against each other. Finally, remove those stems which are hanging out over the ground. When forced into making a choice, cut out the older branch. Remember that a vine may not be pruned after February as it will suffer from severe bleeding.

Prune perennials at the start of each year to prevent any damage to early flowering border plants. Wallflowers and tulips give this flower-border an early display of colour.

Perennials

Tidy-minded people cut back perennials in autumn when the plants begin to look unattractive. People who *really* love their gardens will carry out these duties in early spring!

Perennials should be pruned in early spring rather than autumn since the border will not then be deprived of their fallen leaves. These rotting leaves not only provide the soil with nutrients but also give plants and bulbs good winter protection.

A border covered in snow or full of dead flower stems decked in frost is a beautiful sight. Spring pruning is also better for birds and hedgehogs, as excellent shelter can be found amongst uncut perennials.

Beauty in autumn: spiders webs in uncut seed-heads.

Right: I am not at all tempted to cut down this Hosta sieboldiana 'Elegans' too quickly in the autumn. Each season has a beauty of its own.

Pruning for the more advanced

The previous chapter set out a few simple pruning rules. If you are still enjoying pruning after having put those rules into practice, you may now like to consider yourself more advanced and ready to take on the advice given in this chapter.

Trees are hugely adaptable: the fencing does not seem to have posed any restrictions for the tree.

A general list of rules

A few generally applicable rules are as follows:

- Pruning *never* involves keeping the size of a shrub or tree within a certain limit. Trees or shrubs should be replaced by smaller species if they become too big.
- The uppermost bud is the first to produce growth after pruning. Therefore, pruning can determine the direction new shoots are to grow. Pruning branches just above outward-facing buds will create an open, well aired shrub.
- Never prune back more than one third of a bush or tree. Some of the roots will have to be cut back as well if, for some reason, more drastic pruning action needs to be taken. This will maintain an equal balance between roots and branches. Ensuring a good balance above and below ground goes some way towards preventing the growth of water shoots.
- To avoid cutting leaves in half, do not clip large-leafed plants (especially evergreens) with hedging shears. The brown edges which then appear on the leaves spoil the plant's appearance.
- The most important aspect of thinning out a shrub is to remove the innermost branches to allow the plant to "breathe."
- Always use tools with keen edges. Blunt tools cause serious injuries. Large, ragged wounds increase the chances of infection.

Pruning trees

Not so very long ago, trees were usually pruned in their resting period – winter. However, injuries incurred from winter pruning do not heal, which makes trees more prone to risk of infection. Treating the wounds with anti-canker paints went some way to alleviate this problem. Nowadays, it is more usual to prune trees in summer once the leaves have formed. Wounds heal quickly in summer, making the use of paints or stains unnecessary. However, the disadvantage of summer pruning is that the branch structure is not so clearly visible, particularly with regard to shrubs. On the other hand, the pruning required to keep the crowns of larger trees in shape can be judged just as easily in summer as in winter.

An early start has to be made on pruning trees up to create the crown and clean leg of a standard.

Small wounds

Trees lining avenues or walkways should have the laterals removed regularly from their trunks. This involves sawing off the tree's lowest branches. Room is thus made for herbaceous plants to grow under the tree, as well as shade-tolerant shrubs. Use a pruning saw with a sharp blade. Saw off the branch at a slight angle only, leaving as small a wound as possible. The choice must be made between making the smallest wound possible and cutting the branch as close to the trunk as you can. The wrinkled bark found in the axil (or the crotch between trunk and branch) should not be sawn away. This helps the wound heal over more quickly.

Ornamental trees need regular thinning out just like shrubs. Too

A wound which is healing badly because the sawing was too flush with the trunk.

35

The trees will not spoil the view from the summer-house once properly crowned up.

much pruning back will encourage many new shoots – the so-called "water shoots." Therefore, do not be too rigorous. The real expert prefers to wait until after flowering before pruning, although this is not absolutely necessary: flowering will not be seriously affected if maintenance is regular.

This tree was left unpruned at an early stage. Now that it has become so substantial, the removal of the lateral branch seen near ground level would create far too great a wound.

Treating wounds

As stated previously, treating wounds is not always necessary. However, wounds can sometimes look ugly when in a clearly visible position. Treat such wounds with a moss-coloured lacquer. Remember that you are not doing this for the tree's sake but for aesthetic reasons. The use of such substances as tar or even creosote is strictly forbidden.

Pruning shrubs

Shrubs or bushes have different growth patterns and so require differing pruning techniques.

Grafted shrubs

Suckers often grow from the natural rootstock of grafted shrubs. Mutations back to type also occur. Rootstock suckers can usually be recognized immediately from their growth pattern or leaf colour, which are different from those of the cultivated plant. Remove suckers as close to their origin as possible. It is sometimes necessary to remove some of the soil from around the plant to find the source of these shoots.

Evergreen shrubs There is no basic difference between pruning evergreen and deciduous shrubs, but the results of bad pruning will show up less in winter in evergreens as their branching structures are not visible. Do not use hedging shears to clip evergreen shrubs as their leaves are soon cut in half. Ragged leaves with brown edges are not an attractive sight.

Deciduous shrubs which flower on current growth A distinction must be made between shrubs that flower on wood formed in the current year and those that flower on wood from the previous season. To help make this distinction, remember (as a rule of thumb) that shrubs which flower in late summer do so on shoots formed that year – in other words, current growth.

Deciduous shrubs which flower on last season's wood All the early flowering shrubs produce flowers on wood which grew in the previous season. Pruning away several branches from these shrubs will mean a consequent decrease in the number of flowers produced the following season. The usual advice is to prune these shrubs after they have flowered. However, my advice is to prune all shrubs at the same time in spring. In a well maintained garden, no more than a few branches should ever need removing from any shrub, and this will not cause a serious decline in the number of flowers.

Pruning and "stopping" conifers The pruning appropriate to a specific conifer depends on whether it is best suited for planting as hedging or as an individual specimen. To a

A number of the smaller maple species can be clipped into sphere-topped standards or pollarded.

A lime which has been clipped into levels is now ready for summer pruning.

large extent, a conifer's natural growth pattern – conic, rounded, or spreading – determines the correct pruning technique.

Hedging conifers

Crowning trees up into standards is unnecessary under natural conditions: light deprivation caused by surrounding trees results in the lower branches dying off by themselves.

The "stopping" of young conifers takes place in February. Take the conifer between your knees, holding on tightly to the apex, and, with your right hand, use a razor-sharp pruning knife to remove all the growth tips from its leader laterals. (A well sharpened kitchen knife does the job just as well.) If you hold on to the apex all the time, this will prevent you from cutting it by mistake. This kind of pruning gives the conifer a neat, pyramidal shape and promotes outward, bushy growth. Once conifers have grown larger, hedging shears can be used to keep them dense and bushy.

The annual stopping of young conifers prevents their laterals competing with the apex. If laterals are left to grow along with the apex (ultimately becoming metres tall), they may be severely bent down by snow and the hedge will then have to be held upright with ropes or wires. For this reason, common yew, *Taxus baccata*, is preferable to *Taxus media* 'Hicksii' as a hedger.

Once conifers have reached full maturity they can be clipped as often as you like; twice each growing season is the very minimum. When a hedge is not clipped sufficiently it will become too wide and cannot be made narrower again. Replacing the hedge with young conifers will be the only option. Avoid this by pruning regularly. Most people think that conifers require very little maintenance, but this is completely untrue. I should also like to dispel another popular misconception about conifers, once and for all. It is quite false that topping a conifer will cause it to die or that this will make its base grow bushier. Lawson cypress (*Chamaecyparis lawsoniana* 'Columnaris' or C. l. 'Alumnii') is often used for coniferous hedging, but it is an unsuitable candidate: its base always becomes bare. Western red cedar (*Thuja plicata*) is a much better choice. If, in spite of everything, the base of a hedge does become bare, the only remedy is to plant something in front of it.

If a young tree that has been crowned up into standard shape seems a little bare, plants can always be placed within its radius to restore some balance.

Tall pyramidal conifers

Many conifers are bought under the assumption that they will not grow into large trees. However, many species grow naturally in forests where they reach great proportions. Their size can be restricted by stopping the shoots, a process that should be started when they are still young. Nevertheless, if it looks as though they are going to grow too large they can always be crowned up. Remove the lowest branches at the trunk, remembering that a clean leg of trunk should amount to one third of the tree's total height (otherwise the ratio of trunk to crown will no longer be in proportion).

Don't forget that the majority of conifers are shallow rooting, which means that a tall, isolated conifer runs the risk of blowing over in strong winds.

Rounded conifers

A number of conifer cultivars are, by nature, rounded in shape. Perfectly shaped spheres can be formed by regular stopping. *Thuja occidentalis* 'Globosa' lends itself well to this treatment.

Spreading conifers

The most familiar spreading conifers (variants of *Juniperus sinensis*, including those from the natural hybrid *J.* x *media*) cannot be pruned into a spherical shape. However, the regular removal of a few branches with secateurs or loppers will prevent spreading conifers becoming too wide. Pruning should start *before* the plant has started to broaden out.

Cut sublateral branches right back to a lateral so that missing branches cannot be seen afterwards. Pruning should be done prudently so as not to spoil the conifer's natural character.

Neglected conifers

A hedge of coniferous trees whose base has become bare – usually because the sides were insufficiently clipped – will not be made any bushier by topping. Such a hedge is best replaced.

If you consider this to be a rather drastic measure, you can always plant evergreen shrubs in front of the existing hedge. You can top a hedge which has grown too tall if you want to, but if a hedge has grown too tall it is more than likely that it has also grown too wide, and so replacement is again the best solution.

Rhododendrons, to whose family azaleas also belong, require little pruning. Owing to the naturally elegant shapes into which they grow, they often form a part of Japanese gardens, alongside Japanese maples.

Next page: Irish yew, Taxus baccata 'Fastigiata' requires little in the way of clipping. Do take into consideration how much it broadens when mature. (Borg Verhildersum in Leens.)

39

If conifers start to form a great many seed capsules, this usually means they are growing under unfavourable conditions. The over-production of seed is usually attributable to poor growth, and so the tree's position must be improved. You might consider improving drainage where the soil is too wet. Limy soil can be made more acidic using peat mixed with acidity-raising fertilizers.

This heather is ready for pruning. These plants can be cut back shortly after flowering.

Pruning heather

Heather, in its more or less natural environment – a heathland – is rejuvenated when sheep graze on it.

The burning and cutting of peat are not regenerative, as new heather can only grow from seed. Needless to say, sheep grazing, burning, and cutting are unsuitable for gardens, being solely used for the maintenance of heathland. However, it is not so much the manner of pruning heather which is important but when this should be done.

Winter-flowering heather

Prune back winter-flowering heathers with hedging shears imme-diately after flowering. Heathers which have been left to go wild, especially species of *Calluna*, can be cut back down to ground level using secateurs. The result of this, however, is a year's wait before the heather flowers again. Prune in early spring to avoid frost damaging the bare stems. Bear in mind that stems which have become too old will not always produce new shoots after pruning.

Summer-flowering heather   Prune summer-flowering heathers immediately after flowering but not all the way back to bare wood. Pruning must always be done individually, one plant at a time, when a heather garden contains many different species. They cannot all be tackled in one go.

Pruning bamboo   Bamboo does not need to be pruned. Dead canes can be removed whenever necessary. This is often difficult to achieve with secateurs when the canes are on the large side. If this is the case, use a long-handled lopper or pruning saw. The problem with most bamboo species is that they tend to become too thick and so need cutting out. The roots are so tough that you will be unable to cut them, even using the sharpest of spades. The root ball has to be prised loose gradually, so that pieces can be sawn off with a pruning saw.

Many species of bamboo have the tendency to lean over at a severe angle when it rains. Outer canes which have grown too close to a path can be cut down or sawn off at ground level. The other canes can then be bound together. Bamboo should never be shortened, as no laterals will arise after pruning. Prune them as you would flowering shrubs: either remove a cane entirely or else leave it be.

Bamboo species have flowering cycles which vary from plant to plant – one may flower after thirty years while another, such as *Fargesia muriliae*, may flower after eighty. Most bamboo species die back after flowering. The chances of their survival can be increased by cutting

Ivy can also be shaped by clipping. These designs stand out best against a white wall.

the canes down low whilst flowering and feeding them through the soil. The flowers are, in any case, not decorative – they look like ears of grain.

Pruning rhododendrons

In the main, members of the rhododendron family planted as individual specimens require little pruning, although overhanging branches can be cut off. Large, evergreen rhododendrons can also be planted as a hedge. These must be clipped regularly. Begin this clipping once the bushes have finished flowering. If you use hedging shears you will increase the chances of cutting many leaves in half, so it is best to use secateurs whenever possible.

The following are some general rules for pruning members of the rhododendron family:

Deciduous azaleas These can be thinned out in the same way as most shrubs.

Evergreen azaleas Remove branches here and there which have grown too long so that the azalea keeps a better shape.

Evergreen dwarf rhododendrons These should not be pruned.

Evergreen large rhododendrons These should not be pruned. If this type of rhododendron becomes too large, it can be cut back.

Pruning climbers and wall plants

All climbers and wall plants need maintenance from the day they are planted. If you were too slack about this in the beginning, then you will not be surprised at having to cut down your plant completely to let it produce new shoots which *can* be trained: do not neglect your climbers.

A number of climbing plants, such as species clematis, need to be trained when still young. If leaders end up sticking out too far, you are likely to snip through not only the laterals but also the central leader whilst pruning.

The furthest protruding stems of creepers can be snipped off. *Climbers with adhesive roots* are the easiest of all climbers to maintain. This is simply a matter of clipping them back with hedging shears to control their thickness of growth. Shoots from climbers such as Virginia creeper (*Parthenocissus*) and ivy (*Hedera*) should be cut away with hedging shears from around windows and doors to protect the woodwork from damage. Regular pruning also stops shoots from growing indoors through window frames.

Trained or trellis shrubs require thinning out and also need tying back each time they are thinned. Keep them flush against the wall. (See also Chapter 10, *"Pruning according to plant genus."*)

Ivy growing up against a wall can be clipped with hedging shears. Do not let it grow over window frames.

Pruning fruit trees

The most difficult pruning of all is that of fruit trees. Nowadays, the pruning done in commercial orchards (which includes such additional activities as tying up branches) is very different from the pruning carried out in private gardens.

Commercial, bulk fruit production is obviously of far greater importance than fruit produced in private gardens. The branches of orchard fruit trees are bent outwards and tied into position, which usually makes the trees look deformed. In private gardens, high fruit yields are perhaps not as important compared with aesthetic factors, and so garden fruit trees are treated differently.

An old pear tree trained up against a garden wall.

Basic knowledge A little basic knowledge about fruit trees is required before you can prune them. A fruit tree's new shoots can be divided into two types, namely, those from growth buds and those from fruiting buds or "spurs." The latter go on to produce blossom and fruit. Fruiting spurs reach only a few centimetres in length and are covered thickly in leaves. The tree's shape can be "steered" by pruning back the stems that come from growth buds. Cutting a growth stem just above a bud results in a new shoot growing from that bud in the direction the bud is facing. As a rule it is better not to prune stems just above inward-pointing buds. Healthy growth and fruiting are only achieved in open, untangled trees.

If a tree is to produce a high yield of fruit (be it apple, pear, plum, or cherry) then the rootstock on to which it has been grafted should be examined at the time of purchase. Check labels not only for the tree's species but also to find out on to which rootstock it tree has been grafted.

The label should also carry a quality grading. This information is important when it comes to pruning.

When should you prune?

The winter pruning of trees can be done in any leafless period between November and March. Not all types can be pruned at the same time because of the risk of infections, and tools should be well disinfected and the wounds given some kind of chemical treatment. Apples and pears are vulnerable to ash canker (*Nectria galligena*), a sickness most prevalent on wetter soils. Apples and pears are best pruned in early spring since the spores of this disease tend to spread out in the first few months of winter. Do not make any large pruning wounds if there is still a chance of frost. In all events, it is better to wait until a frost-free period before you start pruning. The infection of cherries and plums by silver leaf (*Stereum purpureum*) can be prevented by not pruning until after fruiting. These trees take very well to being pruned in early autumn. Growth stems which have grown far too long can be shortened in the summer, but only after the leader growth bud has formed properly; this is usually at the end of July.

Preventing disease

As well as ash canker and silver leaf, there is also fireblight (*Erwinia amylovora*) – an infection which is the most feared of all at the moment. If a pear tree should be suffering from this disease, the leaves

Apples and pears may be pruned back until blossom appears. Bush form: the laterals from a young bush tree are pruned back and bent out. ("The Little Orchard" exhibition garden at Eenrum.)

at the end of its shoots will start to wilt. These dried-out leaves will then turn from brown to black.

All kinds of members of the rose family can also suffer from this disease, including rowans, cotoneasters, and firethorns. These plants should not be grown in areas prone to this disease. Your local nursery will be able to tell you about the prevalence of this disease in your area.

Fireblight and other diseases can be avoided to some extent by burning or otherwise disposing of infected wood. Whatever you do, do not leave loppings under the tree!

Adventitious shoots should be removed from the trunk regularly while they can still be broken off with your fingers.

Tree forms Before making a choice from a range of fruit trees (which should certainly involve taking pollination into consideration), you should first think hard about the tree's growth pattern in relation to the space available for it. Space is usually the most important factor to consider. A fruit tree's final size is not only determined by pruning but also, and more importantly, by the rootstock on to which it has been grafted.

There are slow- and fast-growing rootstocks. Not only are apple trees sold in about five different forms (bush, half-standard, standard, dwarf pyramid, and rounded) but also with several different kinds of rootstock. When selecting a young tree, there will be up to ten varieties for one species to choose from. Only specialized nurseries will be able to fulfil all your specifications. Even then, you may still have to order the tree that seems most suitable for your garden. And remember, you may be able to control a fruit tree's shape to some extent through pruning, but pruning cannot correct a mistaken choice of tree.

Standards

Standards are trees whose lateral branches start growing at a minimum height of 1.8m (5ft 10in). These can be divided into those with rounded crowns, where the central leader has been pruned out, and those with pyramidal crowns with the central leader intact. This last form is particularly common in pears.

Pear trees grow tall but remain narrower than other fruit trees, which makes them suitable for a small garden.

Rootstock and grafting

Several series of rootstock (known as the EM-series) were developed at the East Malling Research Station in England. The M-series, as it was subsequently known, was complemented by the MM-series, which was resistant to the woolly aphid. As incompatibility sometimes occurs between cultivated pear scions and the desired rootstock, mid-section scions are often used. When this method is employed, two grafting or budding points will be seen on the tree: one at its foot and the other just below the crown.

A display bed with trained fruit trees. Trees like these were planted in ornamental gardens in the 19th century. For preference, choose a variety of apple with a bright red colour. (Oosterhouw Public Gardens in Leens.)

Rootstock choice is determined by the desired rate of growth and soil type. As you can see, buying a fruit tree is a lot more than just deciding what kind of fruit you would like to have!

Apple 'Ingrid Marie' before (above) and after pruning (below).

Apple	*Rootstock*	*growth*	*characteristics*
	M 27	moderate	for richer soils
	M 9	weak	small trees
	M 26	moderate	for dryer, lighter soil types
	MM 106	strong	average growth on dry soils
	'Seedling'	strong	late fruiting, used for standard trees

Pear	*Rootstock*	*growth*	*characteristics*
	Quince A	moderate	not for dry or limy soils
	Quince C	weak	sensitive to frost
	'Seedling'	strong	used for standard trees

Fruit trees may be pruned up until they start blossoming.

Plums and damsons	*Rootstock*	*growth*	*characteristics*
	Brompton	strong	all soil types; especially for standard trees
	St Julien A	moderate	for wetter soils
	Pixy	weak	irregular, produces many suckers
	Myrobalan	strong	suitable for standard trees

(The above-mentioned rootstock is also used for peaches, apricots, and almonds.)

Cherry

Rootstock	growth	characteristics
Prunus avium	strong	produces large trees
MF 12/1	strong	produces large trees with straight trunks
'Colt'	average	sensitive to frost when young

An apple on a fruiting spur. A wasp trap hangs alongside the apple to protect it from being eaten.

Pruning fruit trees

The following sections are a guide to how pruning can produce well shaped trees and encourage a bountiful harvest of fruit as regards apples, pears, plums and damsons, sweet and Morello cherries, peaches, and apricots.

Apples and pears

Apples and pears need regular pruning. If you prune regularly, you will almost never have to tackle the heavier branches. You will also inflict only minor wounds, with a consequent reduction in the chances of disease entering the tree's system. Pruning lets light into a tree, and its branching system should be thinned out where it has become too congested. Don't be over-zealous in this, however, or else adventitious shoots will start to appear everywhere. Always prune just above a bud that faces in the right direction, preferably an outward-facing one. The emerging shoot will then grow in that direction. As previously mentioned, fruit trees produce two kinds of bud: growth buds and flower buds. Naturally enough, flower buds produce blossom and fruit. These should be retained as far as is possible. They are easily recognizable owing to their compact growth pattern. Several individual growth shoots can be completely removed where too many are growing side by side. The remaining growth shoots can be pruned back to half their length just above an outward-facing growth bud. Cut stems at an angle just above the bud. This angle should slant down, away from the bud. If too much wood is left above the bud it will die back, and this will become a future source of disease. Once dormant, apples and pears can be pruned right up until the moment they begin to produce blossom – as long as there is no frost. Cordon-grown trees have gained in popularity in the last few years alongside standards. This tree form has a central leader from which only very short laterals are permitted to grow. The fruit thus appears to hang from the main stem. This tree type also requires summer pruning once the leader bud has formed at the end of July. Cordons are always grafted on to slow-growing rootstock. A cordon should always be supported by a stake since its stock produces few roots. The ground surrounding the tree also needs to be kept clear.

A fruiting spur in blossom. Prune as few fruiting spurs as possible so as not to affect the potential fruit yield.

Right: this ornamental almond (Prunus triloba) should not be confused with a true almond (Prunus amygdalis) even though its flowers do bear a resemblance to it. To the left of the almond, the rare Narcissus poeticus 'Pheasant's Eye' is in bloom.

Plums and damsons

Plums and damsons also fruit from wood known as spurs. These are short sublaterals formed on old wood. Leave as many of these spurs as possible so as not to jeopardize fruit production. Young plums and

Trained plum trees.
The sculptor Fred van
Hessen designed this
modern way of
training trees.

damsons should be thinned out immediately after purchase to leave a maximum of five laterals branching out from the central leader. In the following year, prune back the sublaterals which have grown from these branches to about 10cm (4in). Otherwise, plums and damsons need little more in terms of pruning, apart from being thinned out occasionally to let in light. First, remove any branches which cross each other, or which are growing inwards, and then go on to remove any dead wood. Suckers should be removed in summer. If the tree is producing too much fruit it may be necessary to remove some. The tree may also require support to prevent branches from breaking under the weight of the remaining fruit. The summer pruning of trained tree forms takes place in July. This involves pruning back the laterals to about eight leaves in length. Shoots are still pliable in July, which means that this task can be done by hand.

Standard pear with
cleared radius. A tree
is kept healthier when
not left to grow
surrounded by tall
grass. Clearing a
radius around a tree
also lessens risk of
injury to the trunk
during mowing.

Sweet and Morello
cherries

Morello cherries, unlike sweet cherries, produce the majority of their fruit on current growth. Hard pruning will stimulate this growth. Many shoots formed in the current season can be removed, particularly once fruiting is over. Leave cherries with sufficient old wood for their fruit yields to continue unaffected. Standard trees need regular thinning out to let in enough light. Trained forms can have their shoots pruned back to three or five buds. The difference between leaf and flower buds is easy to spot: flower buds are grouped together in greater numbers.

Peaches and apricots

Pruning peaches follows much the same pattern as that for Morello cherries. Nevertheless, peaches start producing excess shoots when pruned too hard. Older branches almost never bear fruit again, which means using the "renewal pruning" technique: remove a number of old branches every year to give the tree the opportunity to produce new shoots.

Pruning soft fruit bushes

Soft fruit is widely grown. These include grapes, raspberries, blueberries, red and white currants, black currants, gooseberries, blackberries, Japanese wineberries, and trained Morello cherries. The following are pruning tips for each of these.

Grape vines (*Vitis*)

People impatient to pluck grapes after only two years are advised not to embark on viticulture: grapes require severe pruning from the very start. A newly purchased plant should be pruned back to about 30cm (12in) from ground level. In its first growing season, the plant should be topped on reaching a height of 2m (6ft). All lateral shoots should be pruned back to two leaves. The central leader stem may be allowed to grow to a height of 3.5m (12ft) in the third year, and the laterals to a maximum of 1m (3ft). Sublaterals must be pruned back to two eyes, as before. Furthermore, all new stems need to be fastened securely. A vine grown in this manner will develop into a plant full of eyes from which many grapes will grow. Mature grape vines should have all

Prune a vine in February at the latest in order to prevent serious bleeding from the stubs. Stems which have not yet become woody can be pruned back in the summer without any problems.

stems pruned back to two leaves above the last bunch of grapes. This will ensure that growing strength is directed to the grapes and not to the branch. Vines can be pruned from the moment all their leaves fall until the beginning of January. Pruned shoots can still freeze in frosty weather. Frost damage can be minimized if you do not prune stems too close to the dormant eyes.

Right: a grape vine growing freely as a shrub in Herculaneum, the town once destroyed by an eruption from Mount Vesuvius. Growing a grape vine in this way is awkward, but the photograph shows that it is possible.

Raspberries (Rubus idaeus)

Most summer-fruiting raspberries demand a different kind of pruning from autumn-fruiting varieties. Prune back the young canes of summer-fruiting raspberries to a height of about 30cm (12in) as soon as they have been planted. In the first season, new shoots will grow from the ground. Canes that have reached 30cm in length can be cut back to ground level in the autumn. The new shoots will bear fruit the following year, and new shoots will once more appear from the ground. After fruiting has finished, the spent canes can be removed, leaving about five new ground shoots per plant. Ground shoots which stray too far from the row should be removed first, thus making it easier to pick fruit in the future. Each year, new shoots should be tied to a wire that has been stretched above them at a height of 1m (3ft) above ground level.

Grape vines can be trained to grow over all manner of constructions when well guided.

Autumn-fruiting raspberries bear fruit on current growth. This means that these plants can be cut back completely in late autumn or early spring. First, however, make certain that the raspberries to be pruned

are an autumn-fruiting variety, before taking any irreversible action!

Blueberries (*Vaccinium corymbosum*)

Blueberries are grown far less frequently than, say, red or black currants owing to their need for damp, acid soils. These berries require no pruning in the first few years after planting. Their shape is all that needs controlling. A stem which is growing sharply inwards should be removed. Subsequent pruning is simply the removal of single, particularly large, stems. Do not prune out young twigs as it is from these that the berries grow.

Red and white currants (*Ribes*)

It matters little whether red and white currants are grown as bushes or cordons in terms of pruning them.

Shoots which cross one another within a bush should be cut out in winter: the bush must remain airy. A few laterals can be pruned back to the main stem if necessary. Several of the outermost laterals that are growing in a horizontal fashion can also be pruned back to neaten the bush's appearance. The laterals can be cut back in summer (end of June) to up to five leaves' growth. This will stimulate fruit yields the following spring.

Black currants (*Ribes*)

Even in winter, black currants can be recognized by their smell. Under no circumstances should these bushes be allowed to become neglected. This would result in wild growth patterns and a drop in fruit yield. Fruit appears only on young shoots. As a result, the whole bush simply needs a little thinning out in winter. The removal of a few old branches from the middle of the bush all the way to their source is usually sufficient.

Gooseberries (*Ribes*)

Gooseberries are suitable for smaller gardens: they look a little more refined than currant bushes. A bush of eight to ten branches is ideal. Always remove the oldest branches when the plant is dormant. Laterals can be cut back in summer to 10cm (4in).

Remember not to plant new bushes any deeper than they were planted in the nursery.

The deeper a gooseberry is planted, the more shoots will start to appear from the ground. As a result, the bush will try to grow ever denser, which means more pruning work.

Blackberries (*Rubus fruticosus*)

Pruning thorny blackberry brambles is not a pleasant task. However, thornless varieties (such as 'Thornfree' and 'Thornless evergreen') make pruning a little easier. Blackberries tend to go wild quickly, which makes annual pruning absolutely essential. Controlling bushes which have been planted as free-standing specimens is impossible. Therefore, stretch out some strong wire and tie the shoots in against this. You can also grow blackberries up against east- or west-facing walls, provided they are supported by a lattice or attached to wires. The stems that bore fruit should be removed completely in autumn.

Right: Many figs are produced through the consistent pruning back by a third of the plant's growth shoots: Figs may not ripen in colder climates

Young shoots which have grown in summer should be left and tied in. However, a few shoots can be removed, if necessary, from bushes which have produced too many.

Japanese wineberry (*Rubus phoenicolasius*)

Compared to the blackberry, the Japanese wineberry is far more appropriate for an ornamental garden and should be pruned in the same way. Indeed, pruning is easier as it produces fewer shoots. The Japanese wineberry likes a much sunnier position than does the blackberry: a south-facing wall is ideal. Young shoots must be tied in all the time during the growing season. After picking the fruit (which appears on last season's wood), the old stems can be cut off at the ground. Unlike the blackberry, these stems will die back naturally.

Trained Morello cherries (*Prunus*)

Trained Morello cherries can be considered here amongst soft fruit. These can be trained up north-facing walls. Stretch out wires in horizontal tiers with a space of 30cm (12in) between them. Cut away all shoots which face behind and to the front of the tree, and tie in the branches to the closest tier available. Branches in between tiers can be removed.

If a lateral is missing at any height where one is needed, make a notch in the bark in the form of a horizontal cut made with a sharp knife.

Do this just above a dormant bud to stimulate growth. The incision will halt the flow of sap and will ensure that the lateral grows at the desired level. Laterals should be cut back in summer to three or five leaves.

Other fruit-bearing trees

As well as the more common fruit trees (such as the apples, pears, plums, and cherries already discussed in this chapter), there are also a great many other fruit-bearing trees which can be grown in your garden.

Hazel (*Corylus*)

Keep a hazel's shape airy by cutting back its growing central leader while the bush is still young. One of the oldest branches can be removed every subsequent year.

Hazel bushes tend to produce a great many shoots that grow straight up from the ground. These must be removed. In the summer, sublaterals can be pruned back to 10cm (4in) on branches that will bear nuts.

Figs (*Ficus*)

Figs are hardy but are best when planted in a protected position, such as against a wall. In colder climates, ripe figs can only be expected in the warmest summers. Young plants need to be trained well.

Always cut back newly formed shoots by one third to leave the uppermost bud pointing outwards.

In older plants, pruning is limited to the removal of crossed branches. Badly frost-bitten stems and dead wood can also be pruned back to the first living lateral.

Considering how difficult it is to train figs, it is best to plump for an irregular fan shape. Tie in the stems whilst they are still young and pliant.

Mulberries (*Morus*)   There are different cultivated varieties of mulberry, both bush and half-standard. For the best yield, a mulberry should be trained up against the warmest side of the house. Buy a bush form and train this yourself. Just as with a Morello cherry, a mulberry needs to be trained using tiers of wires. As the majority of mulberry fruits are borne on new shoots, regular renewal pruning needs to be carried out so that young stems can replace older ones. Renewal pruning simply entails allowing a bud close to the leader stem to grow out, removing the old lateral in the summer or autumn. Sublaterals in the branching system can be pruned back to five buds. This must be done during the growing season.

Kiwi   If you live in an area where kiwis can be grown outdoors, position
(*Actinidia chinensis*)   these against a sheltering pergola or south-facing wall. Give them space, too, as they grow vigorously. Summer pruning is most important because shoots will quickly grow to be metres long. Sublateral growth is stimulated by severe pruning at the end of June. It is these sublaterals that will be the future bearers of fruit.
In most varieties, pollination can only take place where male and

A wound inflicted by a saw which is healing well. This large injury has almost completely grown over after four years.

female plants have been planted close to one other. Male plants are weaker than the females. If a plant dies, whose sex was uncertain, then it is a fair bet it was male.

Always remove adventitious shoots growing from the trunk. Small ones can be pinched off by hand making the use of secateurs, as seen in the photograph, unnecessary.

Sweet chestnut (Castanea sativa)
The sweet chestnut is often supplied in bush form. However, I prefer trees with a straight central leader which I am able to train into a nicely crowned standard in a few years. This takes up much less space than a vigorous bush form. Apart from this, the tree requires no other form of pruning.

Sweet chestnuts flourish in moisture-retentive, sandy soil. If your garden has a clay soil, it is better to plant a walnut.

Walnut (Juglans)
Walnut trees are supplied in bush and tree form. I recommend the latter, as the vigorous, horizontal growth of the bush form's branches makes it too large for medium-sized gardens. Pruning principally concerns removing dead wood. Inward-growing or crossing branches should be removed before February. Walnuts are prone to severe bleeding in the spring as their sap flow begins early in the year.

Pruning roses

Pruning roses is usually not at all difficult. What is a nuisance is that there are several rose groups, each one of which requires a different pruning technique. Therefore, the problem with pruning roses is that you need to know the groups to which the roses in your garden belong.

General maintenance

Generally speaking, roses can be divided into the following groups: hybrid teas (ordinary bush roses to a height of 1.2m/4ft); shrub roses (the larger bush forms); climbing roses and ramblers; standard roses (roses grafted on to short or tall stems); modern ground-cover roses (prostrate roses); species roses; and "old" roses.

With the exception of species and native roses, what all these groups have in common is that they are grafted to rootstock.

Rootstock sometimes produces suckers, which can be identified by their differing leaf size, leaf colour, number of leaves, and thorns. Suckers must always be removed as deeply as possible: reveal them fully by digging, and cut them out at their source.

All roses can be dead-headed during their growing season, which usually involves a cut just above the next five-lobed leaf.

Dead-heading speeds up the formation of new rose buds. Moreover, a rose-bed always looks more attractive without withered petals strewn all over it.

Disinfect secateurs in a solution of formalin or simply methylated spirits to prevent the transfer of disease.

Make a habit of feeding roses immediately after pruning. If you think of the above activities as part of a whole, you will not forget to feed or manure in spring.

This species rose, Rosa longicuspis, *has been tightly trained along wires and is pruned back close to its leaders each year.*

A well pruned rose such as this 'Schneewitchen' deserves to be painted.

61

Pruning times The majority of roses, such as hybrid teas and floribundas, should be pruned in spring, as should polyanthas, remontant roses, and musk roses. March is the best month for this and, depending on frost, this can be done either at the beginning or end of the month. Light frost is not a disaster, but should a serious ground frost be forecast of around -10°C (14°F) after pruning has been done, it is advisable to cover the rose-bed or plants with a sheet or plastic for protection. Container-grown roses should be taken back indoors again in such an event.

Species roses and old roses which flower just once a year may be pruned in spring, although you can spread out your pruning tasks by pruning these roses or thinning them out as early as the autumn. Hybrid teas, floribundas, polyanthas, remontant roses, and musk roses can all be pruned back a little in autumn to give them a better appearance.

Summer pruning Hybrid teas and floribundas have two main flowering times. Old flower stems can be removed every now and then after the first flowering period in June. Spread out summer pruning to make the second flowering period last longer. Pruning is best staggered by simply cutting a bouquet of roses for a vase every so often. Stems should be cut just above outward-facing leaves. The same applies to standard roses.

Rosa banksiae var. banksiae is the only rose to flower on wood two years old. This frost-sensitive rose can only be grown in very sheltered areas or a greenhouse.

Root pruning

Newly purchased roses sometimes have extremely long roots which will not fit even a sizeable hole. Should this be the case, do not bend the roots around the hole's perimeter but shorten them a little instead. Holding the plant in your hand helps you to see whether there are any suckers. Break these off at the base to minimize the chances of them emerging again from dormant buds.

Current wood or last season's wood

Just as with other shrubs, it is necessary to know which roses from each group flower on current growth and which do so on last season's. Only one rose from the species roses (*Rosa banksiae*) flowers on wood two seasons old, and therefore I shall leave this out of the equation.

Hybrid teas, floribundas, miniature roses, as well as the commonly planted *Rosa rugosa* and *R. nitida*, all flower from current growth. Roses which repeatedly flower throughout the season (remontant roses) – like the majority of Bourbon and musk roses – also flower from current growth. Old-fashioned roses, such as the albas, centifolias, damasks, and gallicas, flower from stems which grew the previous year: last season's wood. These roses require thinning out like shrubs, just as species roses do. They absolutely must not be pruned back.

Those climbing roses which flower just once do so on old wood; continuously flowering kinds do so on old wood *and* current growth.

All shrubs, and this applies equally to roses, can have their roots pruned back slightly during transplantation.

Root pruning. Broken roots are cut off during transplantation.

Shrub roses are similarly complex: non-repeating kinds flower from both old wood and last season's wood. Continuously flowering shrub roses mostly flower from current wood, although there are roses in this group which sometimes flower on old wood, such as the *rugosa* hybrids, for example.

While most people remember which rose it was they bought, the majority will be unable to make head or tail of all this as they will not know to which group their rose belongs. Books on roses always list them by group, which helps you to tell from which season's growth your rose will flower – assuming you have not forgotten the rose's name!

Hybrid tea and floribunda (bush) roses

This group of roses flowers on current growth and can be pruned by a variety of methods, as explained below. My preference is for the first two of these. In the first method, you must first remove any dead wood and small twiggy growths. Leave from three to five sturdy stems. Ring marks can be seen on these stems where once there was a leaf. The ring marks have little buds which, in early spring, are hardly visible. Anywhere from three to five buds should be left after pruning; the uppermost one should be facing outwards. On average, pruning heights will be between 10 and 20cm (4 and 8in). A rose-bed pruned this way is immediately recognizable: no single stem will have been cut to the same height. In England, where differing planting distances

Old stems can only be removed using a long-handled lopper when species roses are left unpruned for a year. Cut out about one stem in every three. Cut them off close to ground level.

are often used, stems are typically cut higher than this. A disadvantage of higher pruning is that plants age more quickly.

In the second method, all shoots are pruned back to the point just above where the stock was budded. There are enough dormant, invisible buds lower down the bush to enable the rose to grow into a healthy, vigorous bush again. The bush will flower a little later when pruned back to just above the budding site, but this lateness will certainly be compensated for by the bush looking more beautiful. This method also includes the complete removal of all dead wood, of course. In the third method, all shoots are pruned back to a height of 20cm (8in) using a long-handled lopper. This will not reduce the quantity of flowers produced. A bush pruned this way will age more quickly and will look messier. The densely growing stems will make the removal of dead wood more difficult.

Standard roses This group of roses flowers on current growth. Pruning does not differ greatly from that for hybrid teas and floribundas. The only difference is that standards are much more distinctive, which makes it much more important to keep them looking tidy. For this reason, I would recommend that you follow the first pruning method (see above). The second method can also be used, but the stubs left behind on the stems after pruning can look rather dismal.

Keep an eye out for suckers in summer. Remove any that come from

Do not be too scared of hard pruning roses. Here is a good example.
Shoots are once again growing out well from dormant buds which were invisible during pruning.

It does no harm to hybrid tea and floribunda roses to prune them close to the ground every so often.

65

the leader stem as well as from the roots. When still young, stem suckers can be broken off between finger and thumb. When using secateurs, they must be cut out as close to their origin as possible, which stops further growth by eradicating any dormant buds.

Weeping standards   This group of roses flowers on previous and current growth. Weeping standard roses are ramblers grafted on to standards. Remove dead wood.

Thin stems out if necessary but prune nothing back. Protruding stems can be pulled in towards the main stem with string, which will heighten the weeping effect. Preferably, prune weeping standards after flowering.

Newly purchased weepers can have all their stems pruned back straight away. Although this will be at the expense of the first summer's flowers, it will establish better branching which results in better flowers in subsequent years. Remove suckers in the same way as for standard roses.

Miniature roses   This group of roses flowers on current growth. Prune miniature roses like hybrid teas. It is worth pruning back to three or four buds. This is incredibly prickly work because it involves dealing with little plants and tiny stems. A smaller pair of secateurs is advisable, since these bushes are more densely packed together.

Standard roses look at their best when grouped together. They can be protected in winter using insulating material for central heating pipes. Stems above the graft can be pruned in spring in the same way as for ordinary bush roses. (Uetersen Rose Garden near Hamburg.)

Climbers and ramblers

This group flowers either on current growth or on leaders and laterals from previous seasons as well. It is the most difficult group in terms of pruning because there are almost no hard-and-fast rules to be employed. Established climbers have extremely woody, brown stems with light-green shoots. If a plant is producing green shoots lower down, the woody sections can be sawn off and the light-green shoots tied into place instead. Lateral shoots on young stems can be pruned back to two buds. Only when a bush has become completely bare underneath should more thorough pruning be undertaken. The plant should then be sawn down to a height of about 40cm (16in). There is always a risk that the plant will not flower the same year that this is done, so such severe pruning should be considered only as a last resort. There are slow-growing climbers as well as extremely fast-growing ones (ramblers). The latter do not require such a refined approach to pruning.

The rose 'Zéphirine Drouhin' can be treated as a bush or low-growing climber.

Species roses and the majority of "old roses"

These roses flower on wood a season or more old. They can be thinned out the same way as shrubs. To preserve their natural character, do not prune them back by more than one third each year. The oldest branches must be pruned continually, which includes those in the centre of the bush.

These stems are usually too thick for secateurs and so require long-handled loppers or, occasionally, a pruning saw. *Rosa nitida* and

Climbing roses trained up pillars are easy to manage: they are approachable from all angles. Air circulates better in a free-standing rose.

R. rugosa should be pruned differently. These can be pruned annually all the way back to the ground using secateurs. These roses are often mowed down by park staff, which has no detrimental effect on flowering.

Many species roses produce very attractive hips. Spring pruning is recommended so that this display can be enjoyed to the full.

Shrub roses

These roses flower on current growth or older shoots and stems. A bush can be pruned back hard when it is known for certain that it flowers on current growth.

Thin out as indicated for species roses where there is any doubt. A long-handled lopper is best for this job. Shorten any protruding shoots from the outer stems and remove the oldest stems from the centre of the bush to give it more light and air.

Prostrate roses

This group flowers on current growth. The newest prostrate roses are suitable for lazy gardeners. They have been developed to save maintenance time in public gardens. Flower quantity is unaffected by not pruning them. They can be mowed down after a few years with a lawn-mower. Many cultivars have been developed in many colours, and they vary in height from 20 to 80cm (8 to 32in). The lowest-lying cultivars should only have their upward-growing shoots removed. The larger cultivars can be pruned back close to the ground just like

Rosa *'Bobby James', a* *multiflora hybrid,* *produces laterals* *several metres long.* *Prune these back to* *within 10cm (4in) of* *the main stem.*

Rosa rugosa *can* *simply be mowed* *level. The weeds* *growing beneath it are* *an attractive presence* *in spring.*

Right: Rosa longicus- pus *combined with* Campanula porten- schlagiana. *(Oosterhouw Public* *Gardens in Leens.)*

68

hybrid tea roses. It goes without saying that all dead wood and damaged stems should be removed first.

A sucker's different colour is soon spotted.

Rose suckers Native and species roses grow from their own roots, as do all natural plants. These roots develop shoots or suckers, which, in nature, the rose uses to propagate itself. Suckers like these are unwelcome in gardens. As a result, cultivated roses are often grafted on to a rootstock which produces fewer of these suckers. Suckers will sometimes arise, nonetheless, and these need to be cut out as close to their source as possible. Dig out some of the soil from around the plant and remove the suckers from their point of origin. This also removes any dormant buds which, if left, would mean you performing the same task again next year.

In certain cases, you can choose with old rose cultivars and prostrate roses between those on rootstock and those with their own root system. Grouping several of these roses together in a border will keep down weeds, but the roses will also start to produce a great many suckers as a consequence.

Suckers are easily recognized in ordinary hybrid tea roses. A cultivated rose's leaf is made up of five leaflets, while that of the wild rose typically has seven. There is often a clear colour difference between the leaves as well.

The popular Rosa 'The Fairy' *can simply be pruned back in spring.*

Left: the majority of "old" rose cultivars can be pruned back like shrubs. The photograph shows a rose from the alba group which has just been pruned.

Pruning hedges

Hedges have been a recurring feature in gardens for centuries. Not only do hedges define basic property boundaries but they also quite often separate a garden into distinct areas. However, a great deal of work needs to be done to build up and maintain a beautiful hedge.

In a restored Pompeiian garden, a hedge of Ruscus aculeatus *can be seen in the background behind the lion with acanthus leaves on its breast.*

Hedging history

Hedges are amongst the oldest kinds of property boundary. In the Middle Ages, alongside palisades, walls, moats, and battlements, they formed almost impenetrable barriers. Thorn bushes were widely used. While dense and broad, these hedges were not very high: you had to be able to shoot arrows over them and so they were grown to chest height. Low hedging and higher rose hedges were also decorative features as can be seen in many contemporary illustrations. Espaliers – hedges trained along latticework – are to be found as early as the sixteenth century. Hedges were now being grown far higher. The hedge came to be one of the constituent elements in the formation of a complete garden, and only one single species was grown in the hedge to make it appear as uniform as possible. Hedges were grown even higher in the seventeenth century, and were allowed to grow on unclipped once beyond the reach of shears. Mazes started to make an appearance at this time, and the hedges planted had to grow taller than a man. Previously, mazes had been made from low hedging that reached no higher than the knee. Hedges were also planted *en coulisse* (with alcoves) so that statues could be placed in them.

Hedges, as well as topiary styles, became unfashionable in the gardens of the wealthy when the natural landscape style became dominant in garden design. Still, new applications were found for hedging, and in these times of severe architectural design hedges remain an essential garden feature.

*A hedge of common lilac (*Syringa vulgaris*) at a cottage on the coast of Hiddensee, an island in the Baltic Sea.*

Hedging plants

Many kinds of tree and shrub can be clipped into a hedge. There are several conifers we only know as hedging plants but which, when left to grow naturally, surprise us by becoming enormous trees. A number of ornamental shrubs such as lilac, elder, and jasmine, although not normally used as hedging, are in fact perfectly suitable. Even fast-growing elders, maples, and privet bushes can be planted as hedging, although they do require an extra clipping session each year.

The arching used in this beech hedge (Fagus sylvatica) accentuates the bench below.

Clipping

Hedge clipping should start as soon as summer begins. The first session should start once the first shoots, which start to break in May, are almost fully grown. The hedge can be clipped again once the second growth period has finished, at the end of August.

Some plants grow all through the summer and so require more regular clipping.

It is difficult to tell where the previous clipping left off when the shoots have subsequently grown very long. In this case, wires or strings should be stretched out along the hedge so that it can be clipped level evenly.

An even clipping height for the whole length of a hedge is measured easily where the ground is level. However, clipping hedges in line with a slope is unattractive in formal gardens. A much neater solution is to continue clipping horizontal levels, incorporating steps down or up every so often.

Although it is often recommended that the base of a hedge be kept wider than its crown, to prevent you from clipping into the base too deeply, a vertical line is the most attractive shape.

Many people have the tendency to clip deepest into the base of a hedge, which is exactly what should be avoided. It is much better to keep the base a little wider, which gives the lower branches more light and helps the base produce denser, bushier growth.

Clip a hedge from its base upwards. Clippings will then fall to the ground instead of hanging on to the hedge. This will save time later as well as giving you a better overall picture of your progress. This method also reduces the risk of creating gaps by clipping the hedge too deeply. These gaps will take some time to fill, as the hedge base is its slowest-growing part.

Clipping errors in the upper hedge are less serious as they recover much more quickly.

Do not watch your shears whilst clipping. Look ahead along the length of the hedge. This makes it easier to judge in which direction to go and to clip the hedge in a good straight line.

A guideline should be strung out so that you can be completely sure of clipping evenly.

Use a length of flexible string for preference: a material that stretches slightly will not sag in the middle when tied between two poles some distance from each other.

Stretch out a length of string before you start clipping. A spirit level can be used to keep a check on the hedge's alignment.

How often should you clip? The more a hedge is clipped, the denser it will become. The following list gives the minimum number of clippings required by the most common hedging plants each year:

Formal, clipped privet hedging.

Species	No. of clippings
Acer (maple)	3
Alnus (alder)	3
Berberis (barberry)	
B. julianae	3
B. x stenophylla	2
B. thunbergii	3
B. vulgaris	3
Buxus (box)	2
Carpinus (hornbeam)	2
Chamaecyparis (cypress)	2
Cornus (cornel)	
C. mas (cornelian cherry)	2
Crataegus (hawthorn)	2-3
Elaeagnus (oleaster)	1
Escallonia	1
Fagus (beech)	2
Fuchsia	
F. magellanica	2
Ilex (holly)	1
Ligustrum (privet)	3
Lonicera (bush honeysuckle)	2
Photina	2
Prunus (cherry laurel)	2
Ribes	3
Salix (willow)	4
Sambucus (elder)	3
Symphoricarpos (snowberry)	3
Taxus (yew)	2
Thuja (arbor-vitae)	2-3
Tilia (lime)	2-3
Ulmus (elm)	3

This painting by Jan Mankes shows a hawthorn hedge which was badly pruned in its youth. The upper hedge is very dense but its base is bare.

Clippings To make clippings from hedging conifers and deciduous shrubs suitable for composting, smaller twigs should be thrown on to the lawn and run over by a rotating-blade lawn mower. The chopped-up material which results is collected in the clippings tray, which can be emptied on to the compost heap. This waste rots down much more quickly once it has been reduced in size.

I find it good practice to clip hedges before the weekly lawn-mowing session. The lawn mower then picks up all the fallen clippings while I am mowing the grass, killing two birds with one stone. If your lawn mower has no collecting tray of any kind, then mow outwards from

the hedge so that the mowings end up under the hedge as a kind of mulch layer.

Clipping young hedges

Just like grape vines, young hedging plants need pruning back as soon as they have been purchased to help them form an attractive, dense hedge. Privet can even be cut back by half.

You might think it a pity to treat these nice plants so severely all at once, but there is no need to feel conscience-stricken. It will turns out to be purely for their own good.

When young plants are hard pruned straight away, they immediately start producing a great many lateral shoots at their base. This will grow into a dense, trim hedge through which even cats and dogs will be unable to creep. Whether or not a hedge is solid or has gaps will be best seen in winter.

Hornbeam and beech

Hornbeam and beech are often confused; people sometimes think they are the same species. If their scientific names are used, however, they will not be confused. The botanical name for hornbeam is *Carpinus betulus* and that for beech is *Fagus sylvatica*. Make sure you know which kind of hedge you have planted. If a few of the bushes should die their replacements should be of the same species. People often fail to do this, and this is the reason why mixed hedges of the two species are such a common sight.

The suckers which always appear beneath lime trees can be shaped into cylinders or cubes, to give just two examples.

When a beech hedge (right) starts growing in spring, it is easily distinguished from hornbeam (left).

A denser hedge is produced when hornbeam (*Carpinus betulus*) is topped continuously from its youth onwards. Hornbeam is also available in an erect form that has a beautifully straight trunk (*Carpinus betulus* 'Fastigiata'). This is a grafted cultivar which can be used to create a hedge 4m (13ft) high but which, nonetheless, will never become wider than 30cm (12in).

Topping *Carpinus betulus* 'Fastigiata' is out of the question if you want to grow an attractive hedge.

A hedge such as this should not be underplanted, as this grafted cultivar is much more expensive than common hornbeam.

A hedge of Carpinus betulus *'Fastigiata.' This cultivar drops all its leaves in winter as compared with the type species. The flowering perennial is* Bergenia *hybr. 'Glockenturm.'*

Clipped, columnar hornbeam, box, and yew (Oosterhouw Public Gardens, Leens).

Special kinds of pruning

When we look back in history we come across all kinds of pruning techniques and styles. Some of these are purely decorative while others are for creating boundaries or improving fruit yields.

Bonsai Bonsai is a method of cultivation where nature is mimicked in miniature. This might involve a single tree but could just as well involve several to make up a wooded glade. Bonsai involves shaping, maintenance pruning, leaf pruning, and root pruning. Bonsai trees can be shaped to your own specifications purely and simply through pruning. Other techniques such as bending out and tying in can also be carried out in combination with the pruning. However, these techniques are beyond the compass of this book.

An old, trained lime tree.

Shaping The nice thing about bonsai pruning is that you can decide which is to be the front of the tree just by turning it around until you have found its best side. Pruning bonsai trees involves choosing a particular form, for example a pyramidal shape, and then carrying out the same procedure in miniature as you would in the garden on a larger scale: removing inward-growing and crossed branches. However, in contrast to the pruning practised in gardens, it is usual in bonsai to remove any branches that are growing straight out or up. This is done to keep the bonsai tree open, making its branching structure clearly visible.

Maintenance pruning Maintenance pruning involves pruning back young shoots while they are still growing and thinning out any surplus twigs. Dormant buds need to be activated by pruning. Remember that the uppermost bud is the one most likely to break; therefore, the direction in which new branches grow is under your control. Outward-facing buds are best left alone because any new shoots growing from them will grow outwards too.

Leaf pruning

Leaf pruning is appropriate for a number of plant species. The purpose of leaf pruning is to stimulate the axiliary buds into breaking. This kind of pruning results in many shoots with smaller leaves. Most species tolerate leaf pruning well, with the exceptions of beech and birch.

Root pruning

Root pruning is necessary to maintain a balance between the upper and lower sections of a tree and to establish a balanced growth pattern. To this end, young trees should have their roots washed clean and their main roots (tap roots) removed. The longer roots can be pruned back as well. Some soil should be left attached to coniferous trees' roots, but here again the tap root should be cut back as far as is possible. Older trees should be removed from their pots every few years and their roots trimmed back by no more than one third of their length. This procedure will maintain a good balance between roots and branches.

Berceaux

Murals and mosaics have been found in Pompeii that depict colonnades covered in grape vines. Latticework frames supported by poles and joined together by laths and joists were common in the Middle Ages. These constructions were for training fruit trees and grape vines.

Latticework colonnades along which and over which plants were trained remained in use until the seventeenth century when the famous landscape gardener Le Nôtre built colonnades of brick and stone. When such colonnades are made by using pruned trees alone, they are known as *berceaux* (covered walkways). In the seventeenth century, the trees most commonly used for berceaux were lime (*Tilia*), elm (*Ulmus*), hornbeam (*Carpinus*), and beech (*Fagus*). Extraordinary walkways were made in England from yew (*Taxus*). Later on, it was not uncommon for these "tunnels" to be made with fruit trees, such as pears, and ornamental plants, such as climbing roses and laburnum. The laburnum berceau at Bodnant Gardens in Wales is world famous.

Until the twentieth century, it was not considered fitting for a lady in society to have a sun-tanned skin. Sitting out on the patio was not the done thing. When the sun shone, ladies would walk with a parasol. The introduction of berceaux and summer-houses meant that these ladies could also walk through gardens without the need of a parasol. Openings in these foliage-covered tunnels provided views of the garden.

The hedging surrounding this boscage in Herrenhausen is pruned with the aid of scaffolding.

Boscage   Boscage is a wooded area through which paths run encircled by high hedges. Large-sized areas of boscage were called "rooms," while the smaller ones were called "cabinets." Beautiful examples are often found in old, baroque gardens. Such high hedging requires scaffolding in order to clip it.

Mazes   A maze is a garden or part of a garden formed by paths running between hedges in the form of a labyrinth. Mazes are principally designed for amusement, the aim being to find your way to the centre and out again from amongst all the misleading possibilities. The hedging required for mazes needs, preferably, to be evergreen and slow growing. Yew, holly, and beech are best for this purpose. They provide hedges which are not only tall enough but which also cannot be seen through even in winter, since these species do not shed their leaves. Privet is unsuitable as it needs clipping more than once a year. Keeping a maze in condition is extremely labour intensive, which is the reason why more mazes nowadays are razed to the ground than are laid out as new.

Labyrinths are well known in Greek mythology. In the story of Theseus and the Minotaur, for example, Theseus finds and kills the beast in the centre of the Cretan labyrinth. He finds his way out again using the thread given him by Ariadne.

Later, mazes were incorporated into cathedral mosaics at the time of

This hornbeam carport looks rather like the entrance to a berceau.

the Crusades to symbolize the difficult journey to Jerusalem. Maze patterns in monastery gardens continued to reflect this religious symbolism for a long time afterwards.

This graveyard on Hiddensee island (Rügen) immediately conjures up thoughts of a maze.

Up until the seventeenth century, maze hedging was still fairly low to the ground and mostly concerned showing off the design or pattern. Afterwards, high-hedged mazes for entertainment became fashionable. Mazes became unfashionable during the vogue for naturalistic landscape in the latter half of the eighteenth century, the only ones to survive being those made purely as garden attractions for people's amusement – the ancestors of modern theme parks, in fact.

Low-lying maze patterns can be made from the low-growing box, *Buxus sempervirens* 'Suffruticosa', or from *Berberis thunbergii* 'Nana.' Large-scale mazes are best made with *Taxus baccata*, *Fagus sylvatica*, or *Thuja plicata*.

Espalier   *Espalier* comes from the Italian word *spalle*, which means "shoulder." It is a term used broadly for various types of training. It can also sometimes be used to describe the latticework frame that supports or trains plants.
Espaliers of trained lime trees are fairly common, with their branches trained horizontally along wires or bamboo canes. If you want to

make such an espalier of lime trees, then relatively young trees should be used, about 3m (10ft) in height. Immediately after planting, all branches growing out to the front or back of these trees should be removed. Branches growing out to the sides should be tied in horizontally to tiers of supporting canes, each tier at a distance of 30cm (12in) from the next one.

Give young trees good support after transplanting them. Two stakes and a rope is the method used in Germany.

Making a frame
Take seven bamboo canes, each measuring 2.5m (8ft) in length. Use three of them to make a triangle to which the remaining four should be secured horizontally, each separated from the next by a distance of 30cm (12in). A square frame requires eight canes: use two canes to make a X-shape. Two further canes can be fixed vertically to either side for extra stability. Secure the remaining four canes to the frame horizontally.

These frames are particularly vulnerable to gusts of wind when trees are young, and will consequently require further strengthening when placed in a windy location.

Coppice
A coppice is a particular type of woodland commonly seen in the country. In the past a coppice provided communities with a supply of wood, the tree trunks being used for fencing or firewood. Nowadays, coppiced woodland is usually maintained to conserve its special flora.

Pollarding   Pollarded trees, particularly willows, are another typical feature of the countryside. Pollarding, like coppicing, also served local communities by providing them with a valuable raw material. In the case of pollarded willows, this meant willow switches which were used for a variety of purposes, including the weaving of wickerwork fences and baskets. Nowadays, willows are almost only ever pollarded for aesthetic reasons or to preserve the special habitat these trees create. Pollarded willows offer good nesting opportunities to owls and ducks, as well as to bats.

Trained trees   Trained trees are not only used to make sun-shades for houses and gardens but also for other purposes as well. These days, trained trees are often planted to screen windows from the view of neighbouring houses.

The most common tree for this sort of espalier training is the common lime (*Tilia vulgaris*). The majority of such trained limes have four tiers of branches spaced from each other at a distance of between 30 and 40cm (12 and 16in). Limes have a naturally horizontal growth pattern, and the desired shape can be achieved by cutting away a few branches in between tiers. It is important to remember that the left and right branches of any one tier should never be separated by more than 10cm (4in) above or below the other. The tree's shape will look much more even as a result. The term *pleaching* is sometimes used for

Old, outgrown lime trees have been "restored" while young ones have been incorporated amongst them.

such trees when trained to grow into each other to form a screen or arch. A lattice or frame is needed to keep the branches tied in to the horizontal. This frame can be made from bamboo canes attached to the tree in triangular or quadrangular format (see above).

Arbour avenues   In places where the summers are particularly sunny, it is common to see tree arbours planted in avenues or rows. Trees are planted at regular distances from each other, the branches often kept low through pruning and clipping. A famous example of this is to be found in the Tuileries Gardens in Paris where plane trees (*Platanus acerifolia*) spread out roof-like along the length of the gravel-strewn pathways and avenues. Benches are placed beneath these oases of cool refreshment. Other trees which also feature in arbour avenues include the lime tree (*Tilia vulgaris* and *T. cordata*) and the horse chestnut (*Aesculus hippocastanum*).

Arbours   You might be wondering what arbours have to do with pruning. Originally an arbour meant a grassy plot or orchard but has now come to mean a retreat or bower of overgrowing trees. In earlier days, people often liked to sit out on the grass in the shade offered by orchard trees. A copperplate engraving from 1450 by an unknown Flemish artist shows that such clipped bowers were a garden feature even then. These were clearly intended to provide shade, just as trees

*The dome-shaped acacia (*Robinia pseudoacacia *'Umbraculifera') should be pollarded each spring. Its branches break off easily in late summer if this is not done.*

Left: An avenue-style tree. These need to be cut back to old wood each winter. The photograph shows Platanus acerifolia.

An arbour retreat covered by a white climbing rose in the Menkemaborg Gardens, Uithuizen.

in an orchard did. Plane and lime trees were used for this purpose. In the sixteenth century, dome-shaped latticework constructions appeared over which climbers could grow. These evolved into retreats and summer-houses made of brick and stone.

Plants which serve well for arbours and which require no latticework support include yew (*Taxus baccata*) and the yellow cornelian cherry (*Cornus mas*). Remember that these plants grow slowly and that it will take ten years or so before you will be able to sit in their shade. The advantage of slow growers is that they need less frequent clipping. Those who want to grow a natural arbour without having to clip it can plant Young's weeping birch (*Betula pendula* 'Youngii').

A metal arbour frame at the Oosterhouw Public Gardens in Leens. The arching reflects that seen in the mansion's window frames.

Topiary

We can trace topiary back as far as
Classical Rome. Box and cypress
(*Cupressus sempervirens*) were used for
creating all kinds of geometric and animal
shapes. Nowadays, topiary is once again a
popular gardening style. Pruning requires
that you consider each stem or branch
before making that final cut; topiary
simply requires hedging shears and a
watchful eye over your design's progress.

Taxus baccata trimmed into a cone (the Menkemaborg Gardens, Uithuizen).

Unnatural shapes   Topiary does not take into consideration a plant's natural growth pattern. You do not need the same type of background knowledge necessary to prune successfully, although a feeling for shape and form, as well as the self-discipline to clip plants regularly, are absolutely essential. The only tools needed are hedging shears and hand shears – a smaller kind of hedging shears for more detailed work. Lawn clippers, which look like sheep shears, are also useful.

You could make your lawn come alive with chickens. Real chickens can wreck a lawn and need feeding every day, but box chickens, on the other hand, only demand your attention once a month. Shapes like these can be made using supporting materials such as wires, wire netting, or chains. Clipping guides like these (through which yew, box, or ivy (*Hedera helix*) can grow) give you the opportunity to create anything in your garden up to and including a huge chessboard.

Sun-dials are often costly. Take your time and grow one out of box spheres. English knot gardens are famous. These contain all kinds of box bushes in different colours, which are trimmed according to their colour into low hedges. There are box cultivars with variegated and yellow leaves. Hedges made up of several different cultivars appear to intertwine or "knot" into each other. Try to come up with some topiary designs of your own to add that personal touch to your garden. It won't be the end of the world if it doesn't work!

Topiary history

In Roman times a *topiarius* was a specialized gardener who shaped trees and bushes. Pliny, well known for his interest in gardening, describes topiary in his famous letters. Hedging, typically, was made from box and yew, as well as from broom. Hedge-pruning techniques had already become commonplace in Holland and Flanders by the Middle Ages.

Clipped trees were usually grown in pots. Contemporary illustrations often show trees clipped to form pillars. The range of topiary designs became much broader from the sixteenth century onwards, including a fashion for animal shapes. One of the oldest of these designs was a wedding cake made from yew. The shape was built up in layers. The trunk in between these layers was left showing, and the apex was clipped into a decorative motif.

Early topiary made its greatest impact in Holland, but by the seventeenth century it had become very fashionable in France and England. Topiary's zenith came in the eighteenth century. In Holland and Flanders, single small trees were clipped to form symmetrical designs. The same technique was used in France where the landscape gardener Le Nôtre made topiary a feature of French gardens. Many topiary trees and styles were imported into England from Holland. The gardens of King William III of England (who was originally a Dutch prince) certainly stimulated the widespread application of this

Almost all species of shrub can be shaped by clipping, particularly conifers. Use your imagination.

Buxus sempervirens *clipped into a star shape and* Ligustrum delavayanum *clipped into spheres (Oosterhouw Public Gardens, Leens).*

86

kind of "living art." Topiary became such a craze in England that all sense of proportion was soon lost. Entire parks were devoted to topiary designs, which prevented any appreciation of the garden's original layout.

The fashion for landscape-style gardens meant an end to topiary. Only a few symmetrically laid-out gardens were maintained. Shaped trees no longer fitted in with the "natural look" of landscaped parks, and these were uprooted as a result.

Over a period of fifty years, the shaped trees gradually disappeared from the gardens of the wealthy all over Europe. Just a few remained here and there in cottage gardens. Good examples of topiary can still be seen in cottage gardens today, as well as examples of arbour-shaped plane trees.

Suitable shrubs — Excellent candidates for topiary styles are, in order of importance, *Taxus, Buxus*, and *Ilex*.

Yew is known as a slow-growing tree, but this is not entirely true. Once planted, a well maintained and well fed yew tree will grow very quickly indeed.

Box is a little slower. Therefore, your choice of cultivated variety needs to be considered carefully.

A sun-dial made from box spheres in the Menkemaborg Gardens (North Groningen).

Even common haw-thorn can be clipped to form a dense sphere-topped standard. The density of foliage allows greater nesting opportunities to small song birds.

87

Common box is suitable for the majority of applications, but when making large cubes it would be better to use *Buxus sempervirens* 'Rotundifolia' and for low edging around a border *Buxus semper-virens* 'Suffruticosa.'

Sheltered areas in semi-shade can also be planted with the much more expensive *Ruscus aculeatus* (butcher's broom).

The following shrubs are suitable for topiary and clipping:

Buxus sempervirens (box)
Ligustrum delavayanum (privet)
L. ovalifolium
Lonicera nitida (bush honeysuckle)
Taxus baccata (yew)
Juniperus communis (common juniper)
Ilex aquifolium (holly)

Shrubs which need more warmth

The following plants are not suitable for planting outdoors in colder climates. An unheated greenhouse is the only practical place where they can be grown and clipped. These plants could also be container-grown, in which case they can be brought outdoors in summer and placed on the patio.

Don't forget that potted plants will not tolerate any frost at all, while

Box hedging in the medieval herb garden of the Ter Apel monastery.

Cypress hedge (Cupressus macrocarpa) in a garden in Naples.

plants growing in the soil of an unheated greenhouse are able to put up with a few degrees of frost:

Cupressus macrocarpa (Monterey cypress)
Laurus nobilis (sweet bay)
Myrtus communis (common myrtle)
Viburnum tinus (laurustinus)
Rhododendron japonicum (Japanese azalea)

A clipped Quercus robur *'Fastigiata' next to the Grand Palace in Sans Souci Park, Berlin.*

Suitable trees   When the subject of topiary is mentioned, you might simply have a mental picture of low, clipped designs. People all too often forget that trees can be clipped and shaped just as easily. The following trees are all appropriate for topiary. *Carpinus betulus* 'Fastigiata' and *Quercus robur* 'Fastigiata' are good specimens for clipping into topiary cylinders or pillars; the other trees can be clipped into perfectly rounded spheres:

Ilex aquifolium (evergreen)
Quercus ilex (evergreen)
Taxus baccata (evergreen)
Thuja plicata (evergreen)
Carpinus betulus 'Fastigiata' (deciduous)
Pyrus salicifolia 'Pendula' (deciduous)
Quercus robur 'Fastigiata' (deciduous)
Quercus petraea 'Columna' (deciduous)

Quercus robur *'Fastigiata' exhibiting its natural growth form.*

Quick results   Shaping a tree into a perfect form can take a lifetime. Something attractive, such as a stately column or cylinder, can be produced much more quickly by using x *Cupressocyparis*, a cross between *Cupressus sempervirens* and *Chamaecyparis* nootkatensis. This tree can reach a height of some 20m (65ft).

A disadvantage of fast growers like these is that they need more frequent clipping. An additional disadvantage of this hybrid is its sensitivity to frost when young, which makes it only suitable for milder climates and coastal areas. Many cultivars of x *Cupressocyparis leylandii* are available that have light green or yellow foliage.

Free-form topiary   Yew, box, and *Lonicera nitida* or *L. pileata* are the most suitable subjects for free-form topiary. The design does not need to be worked out in advance: your inspiration whilst clipping can determine what shape the bush will take on. Many free-form topiary designs can be seen in cottage gardens: hollows and bulges which, in time, become ever more pronounced. Essentially, the forms created should be uneven. Anything angular with sharp corners should be avoided completely. Shrubs should be pruned with shears to create a good curving, undulating effect. Hedging and hand shears are the most appropriate tools for the job. Decent hollows cannot be created using electric hedge clippers.

x Cupressocyparis leylandii *is the fastest growing of hedges for areas with a mild climate.*

Sphere-topped standards

Sphere-topped standards are amongst the oldest forms of topiary. The relative sensitivity of a tree's trunk to frost should be taken into consideration if you decide to do this type of work. Insulating material, such as that used to lag pipes, can be wrapped around the trunk in winter to prevent frost damage. Remove soil from around the trunk's base to a depth of 5cm (2in). Wrap the insulating material about the trunk from this point upwards to protect its whole length, including that within the upper soil level. Spheres need clipping very frequently to keep them in good shape. This is best done using kitchen scissors if the trees are still small. The following shrubs are suitable candidates when making sphere-topped standards: *Buxus sempervirens, Elaeagnus pungens* 'Maculata,' *Ligustrum ovalifolium, L. delavayanum, Euonymus japonica, Chamaecyparis lawsoniana,* and *Rosa* 'De Meaux,' a beautiful pink rose which has a more or less naturally rounded form. The dome-shaped acacia *Robinia pseudoacacia* 'Umbraculifera' and the Norway maple *Acer platanoides* 'Globosum' also have naturally rounded forms. The former is suitable for planting in small gardens, while the wide-spreading maple is especially suitable for larger ones. The Norway maple should only be planted in a medium-sized garden if its size can be kept within limits through regular pruning back. The rounded acacia should also be cut back annually to prevent branches from breaking in late summer. And bear in mind that its branches will grow extremely long on richer, clay soils.

Next page: When shaping box, always place a sheet of some kind on the ground to catch clippings. Cut-off leaves turn white when left to lie on the ground, and are an ugly sight.

Japanese azalea is a perfect candidate for free-form shaping.

Several kinds of conifer can be clipped into spheres. The Chamaecyparis lawsoniana *shown here is a good example*

91

Pruning according to plant genus

General guidelines about pruning have been given in previous chapters. This chapter discusses how pruning should be tackled taking individual plants in turn. However, a plant's growth habits will not be described unless these have a bearing on pruning.

Flowers on current growth and on last season's

Shrubs which flower early usually form flowers on branches which grew in the previous season. In other words, they flower on last season's wood. The shrub will not be able to flower on this growth if it is pruned back the winter before. Therefore, winter pruning will decrease flower quantity. A shrub flowering on last season's wood is best pruned after it has flowered.

Generally, late-flowering shrubs flower on shoots that have grown this spring – current growth. These shrubs can be pruned back hard in autumn without affecting flowering the following year. In fact, this can even increase the amount of flowers produced.

Pruning

Try to remember in what season any given plant flowered the previous year. You will then be able to tell whether or not it flowers on current growth or on last season's wood, and thus what time of year you should prune.

As mentioned earlier, pruning has nothing to do with cutting things off because you feel they have become too big. If this happens, the plant should be removed and something put in its place which *does* meet with your height or width specifications. In this chapter, pruning always means thinning out; cutting back is only needed very occasionally, for example if there is frost damage or if a path has become impassable owing to overhanging branches.

Each shrub will now be dealt with in turn as regards pruning

Young shoots growing in the wrong direction can be removed. This lets light and air into a bush.

TIP

If you would like to have a rounded element in your garden, but you do not feel like doing a lot of clipping, then you might like to consider planting a *Thuja occidentalis* 'Globosa.' As the name suggests, this arbor-vitae has a naturally rounded form.

techniques. Since no two shrubs are alike there would be little point in providing a diagram to illustrate how an ideal shrub should look. The "ideal" shrub is only created after years of consistent and correct pruning.

Shrubs with hollow or soft, pithy stems are best pruned after the last frost in spring. Hollow stems can become filled with water, and if this water freezes these stems can expand and split. There is also the danger that hollow or pithy stems pruned in autumn will start to rot away because of the water accumulated within them.

In early spring, sap rises powerfully from the roots of certain woody plants, such as maple, nut-bearing trees, Caucasian wing-nut, birch, grape vines, parrotia, and kiwi. This pressure lasts until the leaves have been fully formed. These plants will bleed heavily if pruned in spring. This will not necessarily result in their death, but the plants will suffer, nonetheless. Moreover, bleeding is not an attractive sight. It is therefore recommended that these kinds of trees and shrubs are pruned in summer or autumn.

Ideal pruning times have been given for a number of plants. This does not mean that these plants cannot be pruned just as well in spring as during their dormant period. If you were to leave pruning to an expert, you would not expect him or her to return on separate occasions just to prune bushes that were exceptions to the rule.

The butterfly bush (Buddleia) is a good example of a shrub which flowers on current growth. This means that it flowers on shoots which have grown that same year.

94

Acanthopanax sieboldianus

This shrub needs little pruning, even when used in a free-growing hedge. A mature shrub can be stooled down to ground level. This is best done using a long-handled lopper owing to the shrub's sharp spines.

Acer (maple)

Maple branches should be pruned before the sap stream starts to rise again in mid-February. Summer pruning does not present any such problems.

Acer campestre (field maple)

Prune this shrub to produce a clean leg if you want it to have it to grow as a tree, or stool it back once every five years if you wish it to grow as a bushy shrub. It requires clipping three times a year when it is used to form a hedge.

Acer japonicum

Pruning could spoil this shrub's spreading form. If necessary, remove any awkwardly protruding branches, but do not forget how slowly this species grows.

Acer palmatum (Japanese maple)

Does not require pruning. Only remove dead wood once the shrub is in leaf.

A single, unwanted branch may be removed in winter. This shrub grows extremely slowly: even a professional will think twice before removing a branch!

Aesculus parviflora (bush chestnut)

Does not require pruning. Its longest suckers can be removed if necessary.

Remember that this plant can become very large indeed.

*A newly planted Norway maple (*Acer platanoides *'Globosum'). The tree eventually develops a rounded, dome-shaped crown if left unpruned. The stake has been attached in the correct manner. The cleared tree radius protects the tree from damage inflicted by insects or lawn mowers.*

*Top: the field maple (*Acer campestre*) is suitable for planting as a hedge and can also be combined with hawthorn (*Crataegus*).*

Left: Acer palmatum's *spreading growth pattern makes it an outstanding candidate for a Japanese garden (the Japanese Garden in Clingendael Park, The Hague).*

Amelanchier lamarckii (juneberry)

This shrub is an ideal specimen for teaching someone how to prune. Crossed branches often occur in this upward-growing shrub. These should be removed as well as those

The butterfly bush (Buddleia) is an exception to the pruning rule: cut the bush right back in spring in order to produce more flower.

branches which grow through the bush from left to right. Remove these branches completely or at least down to the next lateral. In other words, this bush needs thinning out. Since it is not covered in dense foliage, it can be pruned quite easily in summer.

Amorpha canescens (shrubby indigo or lead plant)

Flowers on last season's wood. Only the oldest branches need removing.

Andromeda polifolia

This compact, woody plant is grown because of its beautiful flowers. The shrub itself is not so very attractive. If needs be, remove its ugliest branches.

Aralia syn. Fatsia (Japanese angelica tree)

Do not prune this bush. Suckers can be removed from its base to keep the bush more compact.

Suckers from the variegated form (*Aralia elata* 'Variegata') are always green and should be removed quickly.

Aristolochia (Dutchman's pipe)

If this climbing plant is well trained along wires when still young, all its protruding lateral shoots can be removed efficiently – without fear of cutting through the leader. Allowing the plant to grow freely when young only stores up pruning problems for later.

Aronia (chokeberry)

This will tolerate long periods of neglect. However, it is better to thin it out once every few years. Better still, remove one or two branches two seasons old each year.

Aucuba

Do not prune. Pruning this plant may spoil its shape. There are two options should it become bare: the shrub can either be stooled or else underplanted with shade-tolerant plants. Frost-bitten branches are best cut back to living wood.

Berberis (barberry)

When buying a *Berberis do not* forget what an unpleasant task pruning will be: its spines can even penetrate gardening gloves, and these will quickly injure and irritate your hands.

Formal, clipped box hedging keeps a garden attractive in winter.

The oldest branches from deciduous species should be cut back to ground level annually.

Use a long-handled lopper to help you reach the innermost branches more easily.

Berberis needs to be clipped twice yearly if it is being grown as hedging. For low-lying hedges which only need to be clipped once a year, it is best to plant *Berberis thunbergii* 'Nana' or *B. buxifolia* 'Nana.'

Pruning evergreen species is the same as for the deciduous ones. Branches can also be pruned back. Damage to the branching structure will not be apparent as these species keep their leaves in winter.

The best season for pruning is early spring, or immediately after flowering.

Buddleia davidii (butterfly bush)

This shrub flowers on current growth. After the last frost of spring, cut this shrub all the way back to 50cm (20in) above ground level. Leave a small section of last summer's growth on the branches. This is the only large shrub where pruning is less important than just cutting back.

A bush that is left unpruned will have a sharp decrease in the number of flowers it produces after one year.

Buddleia alternifolia flowers on last season's wood. It can be thinned out in July once it has finished flowering. *B. globosa* also blooms on last season's wood. This species can be recognized by its globular, yellow flower heads. It only needs a little thinning out.

Buxus (box)

Box requires little pruning when grown as a free-standing specimen bush.

It needs clipping twice each summer when grown as hedging: the first time at the beginning of June and the second time in August.

To prevent leaf scorching, it is best to clip box during a rainy period and never on days when the sun is out.

If this is unavoidable, it is best to cover the hedge for a few days with some old sheets. If box is to be pruned back hard, this is best done in early spring to avoid any danger of scorching.

Low, box-border hedging is not the result of intense clipping – it comes naturally from a low-growing cultivar, that being *Buxus*

As far as possible, restrict the pruning of Chaenomeles *to the removal of obtrusive branches.*

sempervirens 'Suffruticosa.' The cultivar *B. s.* 'Rotundifolia' is the best choice when creating larger, geometric shapes.

Callicarpa

Remove the oldest branches from this bush. The continual pruning of branches two seasons old will result in a more compact bush than will the pruning of branches three seasons old.

This bush is often late to start growing after severe winters, but this should not cause concern. Wait until the bush has come fully into leaf before cutting off any frost-bitten shoots.

Calluna (heather, ling)

Older heathers which have become woody should be cut back fairly severely once the last frost is over, but not all the way back to ground level.

Such a rigorous pruning method can be avoided by removing the flowering stems once flowering has finished. In theory, a heather garden requires little work, but pruning does need to be done at the right moment.

Calycanthus (allspice)

This bush needs little pruning except for the removal of a few old branches after flowering.

Caragana (Siberian pea-tree)

This narrow, upward-growing bush should only need to have a single branch removed after purchase if this is rubbing against others. This should be removed at ground level.

Caryopteris

This shrub's branches usually freeze in winter.

The bush should be pruned back to the ground if this happens. It will produce new growth again in spring. The bush can be thinned out after mild winters should the shoots still be alive.

Ceanothus (California lilac)

Prune this bush back in spring, which will encourage it to grow more bushily in summer. This bush often suffers from frost, in which case it should be cut back to the ground.

Scratch the phloem under the bark to see whether or not there is any living wood.

Cercidiphyllum japonicum (katsura tree)

This bush requires little pruning except for the removal of any crossed branches. A specimen with a single central leader is very good for crowning up. Remember that this small shrub will eventually become a large tree.

Cercis (Judas tree)

This tree requires no pruning. Branches crossing others can be removed if necessary.

Chaenomeles (japonica)

Flowers on old wood. This tree should be thinned out annually, and overhanging branches should be removed. Remove a few of the longer branches but prune fruiting spurs as little as possible as these produce the flowers. Intense pruning will result in the appearance of many undesirable adventitious shoots. Therefore, avoid over-pruning.

Chionanthus (fringe tree)

This bush hardly requires any pruning.

Clematis

Much has been written on the subject of pruning clematis. Although pruning itself does not pose many problems, it is difficult deciding to which group a clematis belongs as each group requires a different pruning method. Of particular importance when pruning clematis is to know whether it flowers early or late. In addition, it should also be noted that pruning is only one aspect of clematis maintenance. Just as important is

Clematis armandii *in an unheated greenhouse. Cut back stems which are too long.*

tying the plant well in during the growing season. If climbers have become overgrown and neglected, it is best to cut them back close to the ground. Most of the cultivars will take a year before flowering again after such severe treatment. Clematis can be divided into three pruning groups: Group A (a lot of pruning); Group B (little pruning); and Group C (no pruning). Group A includes the late-flowering hybrids, all the *Clematis viticella* cultivars, and *C. tangutica*. The most well known example from this group is *C.* 'Jackmanii.' *Clematis* in this group which flower from July onwards can be cut back to about 50cm (20in) above ground level.

A species clematis together with a climbing rose planted up against an old fruit tree. The only pruning required is a little thinning out.

Right: larger species of cornel, such as this Cornus kousa, *will not be kept compact by pruning. Give them enough room to grow when still young plants.*

This is preferably done in early spring so that a cut can be made just above the lowest break buds. Early-flowering clematis hybrids with large flowers belong to Group B. The most familiar cultivars from this group are 'Nellie Moser' and 'Mme Le Coultre.' This second group includes those clematis which produce flowers on stems that grow from woody laterals. In early spring, protruding laterals should be cut back to buds, which can be seen clearly when on the point of breaking. Do not cut back the whole plant: it is from these break buds that stems will grow to produce the flowers.

Group C includes species clematis and cultivars of these (with small flowers). The most typical are *C. montana* and, to a lesser extent, *C. alpina* and *C. macropetala*. Clematis species from this group flower directly on last season's wood. Anything pruned from these plants is at the expense of flowers. This is not to say, however, that thinning out is not sometimes necessary. Do not be alarmed by all this. A clematis will not die if you prune it the wrong way, but the number of flowers produced will decrease.

I should like to give some separate advice about *C. vitalba*, traveller's joy, which far surpasses even the Russian vine as far as growth is concerned. This plant needs to be tightly tied in to prevent chaos in the future. The plant can eventually be trimmed with hedging shears without harming its leader. The whole plant should be cut back down to the ground if it grows into a tangle of shoots that prevents you from being able to distinguish which stem is the leader. If the upper portion of a plant suddenly dies back completely during the summer, this is an indication of the notorious "clematis wilt." Any clematis so afflicted should be cut down entirely to ground level. Dormant buds will produce shoots the following year. Remove all pruned material from the site or burn it, thus preventing, as far as possible, any reoccurrence of the disease.

Clerodendrum
This bush does not actually require pruning. It can be thinned out somewhat during the growing season, and any obtrusive branches can be removed in spring.

The removal of a single old branch (cut off at ground level) is all a hazel requires.

*Left: cornelian cherry (*Cornus mas*) flowers in spring when the majority of bushes are being pruned.*

Clethra (sweet pepper bush)
Remove the oldest branch (two seasons old) annually to keep the bush vigorous. Do this in spring to avoid frost damage.

Colutea (bladder senna)
This bush should be thinned out slightly. Remove crossed branches. Sublaterals can be cut back to laterals.

Cornus (cornel)
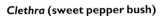
Regarding *Cornus alba*, first remove those outermost branches that are bending down to the ground. Thin out the remainder from the (now) more vertically inclined bush. Branches trailing along the ground often produce roots which can be used for propagation. The cultivar 'Sibirica' with its bright red stems has a naturally

more attractive form and is simpler to prune: thinning out once a year is all that is needed. Its branches can also be cut back down to ground level each year. In contrast, the cornelian cherry (*Cornus mas*) grows extremely slowly when young. Only after three years will it need any pruning. Leave three to five good leader stems, making sure they are evenly distanced from one another. In the end very little more will need to be done. In fact, pruning will be restricted to cutting a few stems for flower arrangements. The majority of cornels grow very tall and require little pruning. Remove only those branches which cross each other or which overhang too far.

Cortaderia (pampas grass)
Leaves which have died back

protect the plant from frost in winter. Only cut away these dead leaves in spring. If the tussock is small, this can easily be done using secateurs. Once the tussock has grown, it will be easier to use a small pruning saw. Cut all stems back to 10cm (4in) from the ground. Depending on the last frost, this should be done between mid-March and mid-April. If the plant produces no new growth this does not mean you have done a bad job: the plant may have been severely frost-bitten. You should have insulated it better against the cold.

Corylopsis
The compact *Corylopsis pauciflora* does not need pruning. The larger-sized *C. spicata* can have one of its larger branches removed once every two years to stimulate the growth of

101

Ensure that Cotoneaster horizontalis *keeps growing flush with a wall by cutting back all protruding branches annually.*

new branches which will rejuvenate the bush.

Corylus (hazel)

Each year, one branch should be removed at ground level from the centre of the bush.

The same should be done with the corkscrew hazel (*Corylus avellana* 'Contorta'). An eye should be kept on the suckers produced by the latter. These are easily recognized as they grow straight through the bush.

Cotinus (smoke tree)

This bush requires little pruning. When young, remove branches

which cross. The tips of frost-bitten shoots can be cut off in spring. The same is true of the flowers once finished.

Cotoneaster

As for the majority of shrubs, a little thinning out is necessary for cotoneasters. The groundcover species should have any vertically growing shoots removed at the point of origin. This helps to promote dense, compact growth. Protruding branches should be cut back every year from *Cotoneaster horizontalis*, which is often trained up walls.

Cytisus (broom)

Flowers on current growth. This bush can be stooled in spring, but bear in mind that bare stems only produce poor regenerative growth.

Daphne

Only *Daphne mezereum* (mezereon) will ever need to be rejuvenated by thinning out. Daphne flowers on last season's wood, but it flowers so early you are almost always certain to prune it after flowering. Remove a few sappy shoots from the centre of the bush. These bushes start to look bare and ugly if left unpruned.

Decaisnea

This bush requires little pruning. Only crossing branches need to be removed. If appropriate, part of a branch can be removed at the next lateral down.

Deutzia

Experts prune after flowering is over. As regular thinning out is an important consideration for this plant, sawing off the oldest branches at ground level can be done just as effectively in winter as in spring.

Diervillea (syn. Weigela)

This bush flowers on current growth and, as a result, can be stooled in spring. The bush can also be thinned out by half each year.

Elaeagnus (oleaster)

The Russian olive (*Elaeagnus angustifolia*) often suffers from lopsided growth. This happens when the bush has been planted in too shallow a manner, and has consequently been blown at an angle.

Pruning one side will make it look more upright. Prune back the young bush's central leader so that it develops a bushier form.

E. ebbingei and its cultivars are evergreens, which means pruning is almost unnecessary. Branches which grow out too far can be cut back. *E. ebbingei* is a grafted shrub and hence its rootstock often produces suckers.

These are easy to recognize at pruning time since they are deciduous. Even in summer they can be told apart: their leaves are less leathery and lighter in colour. Evergreen oleasters can also be clipped with hedging shears to form a sphere, for example.

Empetrum (crowberry)

This plant does not need to be pruned. Young shoots grow over the old ones, giving the plant a perpetually young, shiny-green appearance. Its dense foliage keeps down weeds.

Enkianthus

This bush only requires pruning in its youth to ensure a good shape later. Leave from three to five healthy branches, equally distanced from one another. In the end, the only pruning required will be the removal of any branches which rub against others.

Erica (heather, heath)

Prune heather after flowering. Remove spent flowering stems. The flowering seasons for the various species differ greatly. A heather garden where several species are growing together will need to be pruned in spring, summer, *and* autumn. Plants which

Euonymus *'Darts Cardinal' can be clipped with hedging shears.*

Forsythia is quite happy being pruned whilst in flower. These prunings can be put in a vase afterwards.

Right: the growth of a weeping beech cannot be restricted by pruning. Give it space to grow in when planting!

have become old and woody can be snipped well back, but not too far or else you will reduce the numbers of flowers produced by summer- and spring-flowering species. *Erica arborea*, tree heath, and *E. carnea* do not require pruning.

Escallonia

This bush needs little pruning. Frost-bitten branches should be cut off after severe winters.

Euonymus (spindle tree)

The genus *Euonymus* contains many species which cannot all be pruned in the same manner. The spindle tree (*E. europaeus*) should be pruned annually in winter. Remove only its oldest branches to ground level. *E. alatus* requires hardly any pruning and removing a couple of crossed branches is all

that is necessary. The evergreen climbing spindle (*E. fortunei*) need only have any protruding branches removed. This can be done all year round.

Exochorda

Remove the oldest branches from this bush to keep it vigorous and in new growth. Leave its spreading growth pattern intact. Preferably, prune in May after flowering.

Fagus (beech)

Whether grown as a tree or a hedge, beech is most intolerant of changes to its environment. Changes in water supply or a sudden, increased exposure to sunlight are equally bad for the beech. Bear this in mind when pruning. A clear leg should only very gradually be created when pruning a beech into a tree form.

Prune off no more than one branch each year. Young trees should always be left with a few small laterals, or "feathers," on the trunk to prevent their sensitive bark from scorching in direct sunlight. This is known as "cloaking."

Forsythia

Annual pruning is needed to keep this shrub's rampant growth within acceptable limits.

Remove last season's wood at ground level as soon as it has finished flowering. This creates a low-growing shrub with a good shape and a profusion of flowers. A neglected shrub is almost impossible to get back into shape and is best stooled right down to ground level in spring.

It will take a year before the bush flowers again.

Hibiscus syriacus comes in various colours. The blue variety is hardier and may be thinned out in autumn while the other should be left until spring.

Left: ivy as a ground cover plant requires little maintenance. The border edges need clipping back twice each summer.

Fothergilla

This bush needs no pruning. Removing an old branch once every few years is quite sufficient.

Fraxinus (ash)

Young ash trees need annual pruning: laterals which have become too long will compete with the central leader. Prune back these laterals in time, and ensure that none of them grows above the tree's apex.

Fuchsia

Flowers on current growth and last season's wood. Fuchsias can be cut back to ground level after severe winters.

After mild winters, fuchsias need only have their protruding branches pruned back. They will need thinning out should there be a succession of mild winters. In sheltered areas fuchsias make good hedges. These will need clipping twice a year.

Gaultheria

Neither large nor low-growing species require much pruning. Restrict pruning to the removal of ugly leaves and dead wood.

Genista (broom)

This shrub requires little pruning. Only the late-flowering *Genista tinctoria* (dyer's greenweed) need be pruned back in spring if this seems necessary.

This bush flowers on current growth and its old wood often has difficulty producing new growth. For this reason it is not advisable to cut back too far.

Halesia (silver bell or snowdrop tree)

Only cut away branches that cross.

Hamamelis (witch hazel)

When planting witch hazel, bear in mind that these become large shrubs and that pruning can do little to alter this. It is impossible to restrict its size without harming its form. Remove any crossed branches and any suckers that grow from the ground.

*Previous page: prune witch hazel (*Hamamelis*) in December or the beginning of January so that you can enjoy its flowering branches as decoration indoors.*

For preference, cut back Hypericum androsaemum *in the spring so that its beautiful, black berries can be enjoyed all winter.*

Hedera (ivy)

The bush ivies (*Hedera helix* 'Arborescens' and *H. colchica* 'Arborescens') do not need to be pruned. This is not the case for common ivy. Stems which threaten to grow over door-frames, window frames, and guttering should be cut back twice a year without fail. Protruding stems with flower heads can be clipped back with hedging shears to stop growth from becoming too dense. This will decrease the risk of vermin nesting in the ivy. Ivy can also be trained up against walls and clipped into attractive patterns.

Hibiscus

This bush needs little pruning, which is restricted to the removal of crossing branches and a little thinning out so that more light can reach the centre of the bush. The cultivar 'Blue Bird' may be pruned as soon as flowering has finished. The weaker cultivars are best pruned in spring. A few of the outermost branches can always be removed if a bush has become extremely broad.

Hippophae (buckthorn)

This is a difficult bush as far as pruning is concerned. It often blows to one side and starts to grow lopsidedly. Pruning will help to re-establish balanced growth. A little thinning out of older bushes is advisable.

Holodiscus

This shrub flowers late on last season's wood. It is sometimes advised to prune this shrub after flowering but, because of its tangled growth pattern, the winter seems a better time – its branching structure will be more clearly visible. A neglected, overgrown bush can be stooled.

Hydrangea

Hydrangeas flower on last season's wood, with the exception of *Hydrangea arborescens* 'Annabelle' which produces large, white corymbs of flowers on current growth. As a result, it can be cut down to ground level each spring. For the remaining species and cultivars, all their dead or frost-bitten wood should be removed and, if needs be, they can be thinned out somewhat. In particularly cold winters they may become frozen all the way down to ground level. If this happens, it will be a year before they flower again. Prevent damage by covering them with old sheets or something similar during hard frosts.

A bank of Lonicera nitida '*Maigrün.*' *A choice can now be made. The bushes can be allowed to go on growing outwards or they can be clipped formally, forming an angle of 90 degrees on one side. This will make the sloping side more distinctive.*

Hydrangea petiolaris (Japanese climbing hydrangea)

Pruning is limited to the removal of any protruding flower shoots. Flowering shoots which stick out too far cause the plant to become top-heavy, with the subsequent risk of the plant falling away from its supporting wall.

Hypericum (St John's wort)

The only species that does not to need pruning is the compact, evergreen *Hypericum calycinum* (rose of Sharon). All the other species, which also flower on current growth, should be stooled in spring before that season's new growth begins.

Ilex (holly)

There is an enormous range of holly species. To begin with there is *Ilex verticillata*, a deciduous shrub. This

should be pruned in the same way as jasmine (see below). Only one or two branches should be thinned out annually. If this is done just before Christmas, you will be able to use the branches in a festive arrangement indoors. *I. crenata* requires no pruning, unless it is being grown as a hedge, in which case one clipping each year will be sufficient. If the tips of common holly shoots, *I. aquifolium*, are pinched out each year, these shoots will be encouraged to grow more densely.

The branches of older specimens often become bare. These can be pruned back a fair way, although the bush will not look its best for a year or so afterwards.

Indigofera

This bush flowers on current growth. It can be stooled in spring.

Top: Ligustrum delavayanum *being clipped into a sphere. This privet needs frequent clipping, as can be seen from its fast-growing shoots.*

Left: do not allow Kerria *to become neglected: the quantity of dead wood which accumulates in its centre will mean a lot of extra pruning.*

Jasminum (jasmine)

The yellow-flowered winter jasmine has a display that runs from December to March on its bare branches. Flowering stems can be pruned back in spring. Ensure that this bushy climber receives enough light. Thorough pruning will prevent dead wood from building up.

Juglans (walnut)

Gradually prune up a young walnut tree's laterals to form a good leg

Lonicera periclymenum *can also be trained up a tree and will need next to no pruning.*

until it has attained the correct tree shape (height 25m/80ft). Just like grape vines, prune walnuts early, either in autumn or after the leaves have fallen in winter. Spring pruning will result in heavy bleeding.

Kalmia (mountain laurel)
Pruning is restricted to dead-heading. The woodier parts of older specimens can be pruned back hard.

Kerria (Jew's mallow)
Do not wait until after flowering to prune. A shrub covered in dense foliage takes far more time to prune than when bare. A great deal of

dead wood will accumulate in the bush if left unpruned for a year. Annually thin out these bushes by a third using an ordinary pair of secateurs. This will keep the bush youthful and ensures good quantities of flowers every year.

Kolkwitzia (beauty bush)
This bush is best pruned after it has flowered in June. Cut back a couple of branches to ground level but leave its arching form intact.

Laburnum (golden rain tree)
If necessary, a crossed branch or two can be removed from this tree when still young. Otherwise, pruning is limited to the removal of dead wood.

Lavandula (lavender)
Lavender does not need to be

pruned but will become woody in the course of a few years if left completely unattended. Therefore, it is best to prune it back somewhat in March after the last frost: it then flowers more evenly and looks healthier.

Ledum (Labrador tea)
Do not prune.

Lespedeza (bush clover)
This bush flowers on current growth. This means that it may be stooled in spring. Considering how susceptible this bush is to freezing, it may be necessary to cut it back completely to ground level.

Leucothoe
This bush requires little pruning. Completely remove branches which have finished flowering. Cut them

Nothofagus *as a trained shrub is extremely unusual. Branches growing too far out from the wall should be cut back.*

Left: a lane in a Naples park bounded on either side by Osmanthus.

back to a strong lateral. A few of the oldest branches can be sawn off at ground level if the bush has been neglected. This applies just as much to branches in the centre of the bush as to outer ones.

Leycesteria

Flowers on current growth. This bush's stems can be stooled in spring, assuming that they have not already died back from winter frosts.

Ligustrum (privet)

Privet hedges need clipping three times a year. Hedge plants should be cut back by two thirds immediately after planting to encourage dense basal growth. I know that it may be painful to inflict such severe treatment on your newly planted, 1m (3ft) tall hedge, but you really

are better off doing it! Light thinning out is quite sufficient if the privet is being grown as a solitary, specimen bush. A bush which has become straggly or too spread out can be stooled.

The bush should also be stooled if the branches have been frost-bitten in a severe winter. A bush or hedge will then produce new (and fast) normal growth. Beforehand, however, do check to see that the wood has actually died.

Often it is only the leaves which have been frost-bitten.

This is best checked by scratching the bark: the branch is still alive if there is any green beneath the phloem.

Lonicera (honeysuckle)

Honeysuckles belong to different groups, each of which requires a

different pruning approach: climbing, evergreen, and deciduous. Deciduous shrubs can be thinned out in winter. Evergreens can be grown as low-growing, specimen shrubs, but can also be clipped and shaped. These will require clipping at least twice each summer. Climbing honeysuckle needs to have its stems cut back that are growing out too far from their supporting frame or wall.

This task is laborious and should be carried out in summer. Thin out straggly climbers in winter as their central leaders will then be clearly visible.

Magnolia

This shrub becomes very large and growth cannot be constrained by pruning. Adventitious shoots, suckers, and dead wood can be

111

removed as and when necessary. This is best done in early spring to avoid damaging the flower buds.

Mahonia (Oregon grape)

Remove a single, strongly protruding branch. The bush can be stooled should it become bare. The more unusual species *Mahonia bealii* and *M. japonica* do not need pruning.

Malus (crab apple)

Unlike ordinary apple trees, crab apples require very little pruning.

The majority of cinquefoils (Potentilla) flower on current growth and can be cut back to ground level in spring. A more attractive result is achieved when the bush is thinned out by a third each year. This results in the full rejuvenation of the bush after three years.

Nonetheless, all dead wood and crossed branches should be removed. Crab apples are normally grown in bush form, but cultivated half-standards and standards are also available.

Myrica (bog myrtle or sweet gale)

This bush requires no pruning. Long, arching growths can be removed if need be, as can stems and shoots should the bush start to become terribly overgrown.

Neillia

Flowers on last season's wood. The bush requires a little thinning out each winter.

Nothofagus (southern beeches)

Do not prune. In young specimens, remove a branch which crosses another.

Olearia (daisy bush)

This bush should be cut back to ground level after a reasonably hard winter. It otherwise requires no further pruning.

Osmanthus

This shrub requires no pruning. It is good for topiary work, however: for example, consider using it to make a low, level border.

Paeonia suffruticosa (tree peony)

This plant requires no pruning. Older plants can be cut down to the ground if necessary. New growth will then reappear. Be certain to remove any frost-bitten sections.

Parrotia

This is a large shrub which, at most, requires only the removal of a

Tie back in all climbing and trained shrubs whilst pruning. Tying in was attempted too late for this firethorn.

Top: Prunus laurocerasus *'Caucasica' is best used as clipped hedging. This cultivar is the hardiest on offer.*

Left: Prunus triloba *will only produce quantities of blossom when its branches are all annually pruned back close to the bud union immediately after flowering.*

crossed branch. As with other members of the *Hamamelis* family, leave its natural growth form as intact as possible. When planting, remember that this (expensive) shrub will grow considerably larger.

Paulownia (foxglove tree)
New growth in young trees can be badly frost-bitten. Remove any such frost-bitten branches down to the next (living) lateral. If the shrub is to be grown into a tree, the laterals must be removed from its leader regularly so that a clean leg has the chance to develop properly.

Pernettya
These bushes will remain vigorous if their oldest branch is removed each year. Annually dig in peat around them to encourage the growth of new basal shoots.

Perovskia
Flowers on current growth. Cut the bush down to ground level in spring. The woody parts normally die back in winter because of frost. This does not matter: the bush is certain to produce new growth again.

Philadelphus (mock orange)
This is the ideal shrub for a lesson on winter pruning. It is fairly easy to tell which of the upward-growing branches should be removed. Saw off a few of the innermost branches at the ground. It is often difficult to do this using a long-handled lopper, so use a small pruning saw instead.

Photina
Pruning mostly involves the removal of frost-bitten stems. It is a

good idea to stool a plant hard every so often when its old stems become ugly.

Physocarpus
A third of all old wood should be cut down to ground level. A bush will be completely rejuvenated after three years if this is done annually.

Pieris
Pruning is limited to the removal of dead or frost-bitten stems.

Potentilla (cinquefoil)
Flowers on current growth and old

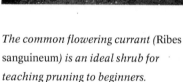

*The common flowering currant (*Ribes sanguineum) *is an ideal shrub for teaching pruning to beginners.*

Top: this azalea has a beautiful shape already without any need for pruning.

Right: rhododendrons used as hedging require more attention as regards pruning. The hedge must be kept dense but not allowed to spread out too much.

wood. Staff in parks and public gardens stool these bushes down once every two to three years. However, it is more attractive to thin out a bush by half or a third every year. This way, you will always have a visible shrub. Thin the shrub out evenly. Use secateurs to cut the stems back as far as possible.

Prunus

The deciduous species are thinned out in the same way as ordinary, ornamental shrubs. The almond (*Prunus triloba*) is one of three exceptions. After flowering is over, prune back all branches to the bud union.

After a few years, this will have produced a beautiful pollarded effect – one of the beauties of this bush.

The large-leafed evergreens are better pruned back using secateurs than hedging shears. This will avoid brown edges appearing on half-clipped leaves. These evergreens can be used as hedging or as specimen shrubs.

Pyracantha (firethorn)

Firethorn can be grown as a specimen shrub. Prune out the thickest branch from the bush, which will help to keep it vigorous. It is best pruned in spring to avoid frost damage. The bush is vulnerable to this, and should be stooled after very severe winters. New growth after that is reasonably certain. Firethorn is frequently planted up against a wall, but few people are aware that this shrub can also be grown in a fan, palmette, or cordon form. Firethorn is at its most attractive when grown as a palmette. Before planting, stretch wires horizontally against the wall at a distance of 30cm (12in) from one another. Then tie in branches close to the wires and remove those branches which grow forwards or towards the wall. This should be done during summer. (See the description given for grape vines, Chapter 5.)

An avenue of acacias in the author's garden.

A reconstructed Pompeiian garden: Ruscus aculeatus *has been clipped to form low border hedging.*

Rhamnus (buckthorn)

To prevent buckthorn from spreading out and becoming a straggly bush, you should cut away its thickest branches each year. Just as for other shrubs, you should first remove all dead wood, then crossed branches, and finally – if needs be – the oldest branch.

Rhododendron

Rhododendrons require no pruning in the first ten years. Problems arise later only if the bush has become too big.

Should this be the case, the bush can be pruned back almost to ground level. It will then produce new growth.

Sawn-off branches fare badly in direct sunshine.

Therefore, protect the bush for a season using either protective gardening covers, or cotton and linen sheets.

Such hard pruning will mean no flowers in the two following years or so.

Many people ask if rhododendrons should be dead headed or not. The answer is that it makes no difference. Tests have shown that future flowering is not stimulated by breaking off the spent flower stems. However, the large, brown seed capsules are not an attractive sight on young bushes, and are best broken off.

Low-lying azaleas, which also bear the scientific name *Rhododendron*, do not require much pruning either. Occasionally thin out the deciduous *Azalea mollis* to prevent its branches from tearing at each other, and also to give the bush more light and air.

Rhus (sumach)

Little needs to be pruned from this bush. However, the annual removal of suckers which can appear from the ground many metres from the trunk is a necessary task.

The development of this plant's beautiful, red panicles of flowers has nothing to do with pruning; it depends purely on the species.

Ribes

Just like the juneberry and mock orange, this is an ideal shrub for a lesson on pruning. All the stems grow from a central position at ground level. First of all, remove any stem which rubs against another. If a fairly large injury has been inflicted as a result of this rubbing, both stems will have to be sacrificed.

Stems which protrude too far also

Prune willows bearing decorative catkins in late spring.

Right: overhanging branches have been removed from this elder. Its leader stems can be thinned out somewhat in a year's time.

need pruning back to a lower lateral or to ground level. Afterwards, you will be able to see for yourself whether any further thinning out is necessary.

As a rule of thumb, no more than one third of the total number of stems should ever be removed at one time. The shrub should look lighter and more airy after pruning. For healthy growth, the leaves within a bush must receive sufficient light. Pruning will result in a more densely growing bush.

Robinia (false acacia)

On rich soils false acacias will grow like wildfire. This means that stems which have just become woody will still be sappy when the first summer storms make an appearance. As a result, many young stems will split and break off.

The tree will have to be attended regularly throughout the summer. False acacias, therefore, are not really suited to richer, clay soils. The dome-shaped form of acacia (*Robinia pseudoacacia* 'Umbraculifera') can be cut back to just above the bud union each spring. This helps the tree to remain nicely rounded, and consequently it will be less vulnerable to wind damage.

Rosa (rose)

See Chapter 6, "*Pruning roses,*" for details of pruning.

Almost all roses flower on current growth or last season's wood. The great exception to this rule is *Rosa banksiae*. This rose flowers on wood two seasons old and should not, therefore, be hard pruned. *R. banksiae* and its many

cultivars are rarely planted in areas prone to hard winters because of their great sensitivity to frost.

Rubus (ornamental bramble)

Unlike the edible blackberry, ornamental brambles are listed under shrubs.

Prune an ornamental bramble as you would a shrub that flowers on last season's wood.

In other words, thin it out in winter. It is hard to make out this shrub's branching structure when it is covered in its lime-green foliage.

Ruscus (butcher's broom)

This is a bushy, evergreen plant with spine-tipped, flattened stems that look just like leaves. Small, white, lilylike flowers are found in the centre of these "leaves." A specimen plant does not need pruning, but this plant can be clipped to create low hedging, an idea which goes back all the way to Roman times.

Salix (willow)

Species of willow with attractively coloured branches can be stooled in spring. The species with pretty catkins can be stooled close to the ground somewhat later in spring, after flowering has finished. These pruning recommendations also apply to the smaller species of willow. Large willows are an unsuitable choice for most gardens.

Sambucus (elder)

Elder bushes can be stooled annually to prevent them from outgrowing other bushes. In one year, new growth can reach a height of 2m (6ft). As elder produces flowers on wood from the previous season, flowering will be reduced. However, annual thinning out will result in the bushes continuing to flower well. The leader stems of older, straggly bushes do look quite attractive, and these can be left with only seriously overhanging branches being pruned back. This helps give the bush a more treelike appearance. Ground elder (*Sambucus ebulus*) is an exception. This bush should be pruned back to ground level in spring.

Skimmia

This bush requires no pruning. However, you can always snip off some short stems with flower buds for decorative Christmas wreaths.

Sorbaria

This tall shrub requires only a little thinning out. You will be able to see just how far the branches bend over during wet weather. These overhanging branches should be pruned back a little. Suckers are a bigger problem, and need to be removed once a year to stop the whole shrubbery from becoming over-run by *Sorbaria*. These suckers are easily transplanted elsewhere. Do this before the leaves have formed.

Lilac always has two terminal buds. This is why there are usually two flowers at the end of each shoot. Buds pointing inwards should be removed in young bushes to create a more attractive, open plant.

Adventitious shoots, even when growing half way up a lime tree's trunk, can be clipped into a topiary design.

Top: these little yew trees will eventually become a level, clipped hedge running the length of the grass (Oosterhouw Public Gardens, Leens).

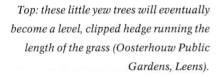

Right: pleached lime trees protect this house from bright sunlight. This "hedge" should be clipped twice a year.

Spiraea

This is a large genus containing many species, so keep a good check on which plants flower on current growth and which on last season's wood. Species which flower late, from July onwards, usually do so on new shoots. Early-flowering species do so on stems and branches which grew the previous year. Late-flowering species can be cut back to just above ground level. These species may also be thinned out. Half of all branches should be cut back to ground level. After two years, you will have a rejuvenated bush.

It's best to remove no more than a third of branches from bushes which flower on last season's wood. This ensures that the bush continues to flower well, and it will be completely rejuvenated after three years.

Staphylea (bladder nut)

This bush requires little pruning and can be lightly thinned out once every few years. Shoots growing from the ground do need to be removed.

Stephanandra

Little needs to be pruned from these tangled bushes. Old shrubs can be stooled down completely if necessary.

Symphoricarpos (snowberry)

The snowberry should be thinned out annually by removing a third of its branches at ground level. This should be done in early spring so that its berries can be enjoyed in autumn and early winter. These bushes can also be clipped and shaped, for example to create a level hedge about 1m (3ft) in height. A topiary or clipped snowberry will produce fewer berries.

Syringa (lilac)

In young lilacs it is best to remove the innermost of the two terminal buds at the end of a shoot. This helps the plant develop a bushier growth pattern. Pruning older shrubs is little more than the

118

Wisteria floribunda *entwines itself in a clockwise direction following the sun. This plant is quite able even to climb around a slippery drainpipe. Left: the scaffolding frame in the background has been erected for a* Wisteria floribunda *(Oosterhouw Public Gardens, Leens).*

removal of dead wood. Lilac often becomes surrounded by suckering shoots, which should be removed each year as close to their source as possible.

Young bushes can be dead headed. While not improving flowering the following year, this will certainly make them look a lot neater.

Tamarix (tamarisk)

This shrub has no set shape, which makes it hard to suggest pruning guidelines. *Tamarix parvifolia* and *T. tetandra* flower on last season's wood; stooling is, therefore, not recommended for these plants, although you should cut off one or two of the older branches at ground level. You are better off not planting these two tamarisks if you want a neat and tidy garden where shrubs can be pruned into disciplined

shapes. *T. pentandra*, on the other hand, flowers on current growth and can be stooled in spring. This bush looks particularly attractive after pruning.

Taxus (yew)

Little can go wrong when pruning *Taxus baccata*: a tree or bush produces new growth even when pruned too hard. In fact, a wide yew hedge can be clipped back close to its central leader, from which adventitious buds will start to break. Drape tarpaulin or old sheets over these bushes after pruning to prevent sun scorch.

T. media 'Hicksii' is unsuitable for hedging or as a solitary specimen bush. Its vertical branches tend, later in life, to bend outwards, and are quite unable to support any falls of snow.

Teucrium (germander)

This compact bush can be trimmed with hedging shears in spring. It soon becomes straggly and bare at its base if left unpruned.

Tilia (lime or linden)

Older lime trees develop large overhanging branches. To make underplanting possible, it may be necessary to thin out these branches or even to remove them completely. You should be aware, however, that in so doing you will lose part of the tree's character for ever.

Adventitious shoots and suckers often appear around the base, or bole, of lime trees. You can cut them all the way back, of course, but it is more attractive to prune them only partially. This dense basal growth can be clipped and shaped into a cylinder or cube, for example.

Cut off firethorn branches which protrude too far from a wall. A bush which has been pruned back level displays its flowers and berries far better.

Right: Fraxinus excelsior *'Aurea' is the slowest-growing ash tree. Older ash trees require virtually no further maintenance.*

Ultimately, it will also be possible to create another such clipped design around the mid-section of the tree's trunk.

Ulex (gorse)

This is a tiresome shrub to prune because of its many spines. Prune in spring to prevent frost damage. The bush will stay fairly tidy if a few of its branches are removed each year.

Ulmus (elm)

Prune this tree as you would other trees. If a tree has become affected by Dutch elm disease, you should immediately strip the bark from the larger branches or, if possible, keep them immersed in water to prevent it from spreading. These branches can also be made straight away into woodchips or even burnt.

If logs for firewood are kept outdoors, you will be creating a breeding ground for the bark beetle (*Scolytus scolytus*) which causes the problem.

Vaccinium (bilberry, blueberry, and cranberry)

Low-lying species need little pruning. The larger high-bush blueberry of North America, on the other hand, does need some annual thinning out to give its berries enough light to develop and ripen.

Viburnum (guelder rose)

The pruning of evergreen viburnum is unnecessary as far as flowering is concerned. Limit the pruning of evergreen species to those branches which hang over paths. *Viburnum opulus* (guelder rose) and *V. x bodnantense* should be thinned out now and then, and any branch which crosses others should be removed.

Weigela

Weigelas flower on last season's wood and so require annual thinning out.
Strictly speaking, this should be done after flowering but if you prune these bushes regularly they can be thinned out just as well in spring. Remove the oldest branch from the centre of a bush and prune back any branches which protrude too far.

Wisteria

At the beginning of July, a fully grown wisteria should have its lateral growth shoots pruned back hard. This can be done until the end of August.

In young plants, you will need these same laterals to train the plant up or along a support. A young plant's trained laterals should be left to grow, while the others should be pruned back to three or so buds. Flowering shoots should be left untouched as far as possible if you want a good display.

Take the immediate environment into account before planting a wisteria. The clockwise, corkscrew growth of *Wisteria floribunda* is splendid for a pergola. Its long, drooping bunches of flowers, which can reach 45cm (18in) in length, look much more impressive when given the chance to hang freely. The disadvantage with this species is that it takes many years before it starts to flower. The anti-clockwise twining *W. sinensis* has smaller bunches of flowers and is

consequently good for wall training. Stretch several wires horizontally along a wall at 30cm (12in) intervals. After a few years, the branches which have been trained horizontally will flower better than those trained vertically. This climber can also be grown as a standard if no suitable wall is available for training. You should train the climber up a pole about 2m (6ft) in height. The leader can be topped once it grows above the top of the pole.

If you prune the wisteria in the same way as a wall-trained specimen, you will end up with a rounded bush covered in bunches of flowers that hang decoratively from its underside. The violet-pink *W. x formosa* 'Issai' is the most suitable candidate for pruning into a rounded shape such as this.

Rosa banksiae *var.* banksiae *in the Oosterhouw Public Gardens' orangery. Its unscented flowers appear in April.*

Zelkova

This plant is usually supplied in bush form. It should have its laterals pruned to produce a clean leg. This will prevent the spreading branches from growing too close to the ground. After a few years, you will be able to remove laterals to a height of 2m (6ft) up the leader stem.

Pruning house and container-grown plants from A to Z

House plants that grow vigorously do sometimes require pruning, but all too often they are positioned in places where they grow only poorly – we can count ourselves lucky that they are alive at all!

A number of container-grown plants need to be pruned back before they are put into winter storage. Apart from that, very few house and container-grown plants ever need pruning as a result of having grown too large.

Obviously, woody and shrubby pot plants can be pruned like garden shrubs: in particular, they should be thinned out by cutting off their innermost shoots at the base.

It is worth mentioning that you should dead head all plants continuously so that they concentrate their energies on forming new flower buds and not on forming seeds. This also gives them a neater appearance.

Abutilon *will continue to produce flowers for a long time throughout the season.*

Abutilon   Treat in the same way as African hemp (*Sparmannia*).

Adiantum (maidenhair fern)   Completely cut back a maidenhair fern in early spring. This fern requires high humidity; foliage will die back in a room with a dry atmosphere. Cut off any dead foliage, cover the plant with a polythene bag to keep the humidity constant, and then find a more humid spot for the fern to stop it from dying back again.

Arbutus (strawberry tree)   In colder climates this plant is usually grown in greenhouses or in pots. If the plant should be frost-bitten – in spite of all your efforts – it is best to wait for new growth to appear before you start to prune.

Adiantum raddianum

This makes pruning back to the correct point much easier. Dormant
buds on old wood can be relied on to produce new growth.

Datura

Bougainvillea   Stems which have grown too long can be pruned back. Regular
topping will result in dense, bushy growth.

If this plant is being grown in a hothouse, you can leave a few leader
stems and just prune back slightly their laterals. *Bougainvillea* can
also be trained, in which case the laterals can be cut back to two or
three buds from the leader stem.

Bouvardia   Remove frost-bitten shoots if the plant has suffered badly whilst
overwintering in the greenhouse.

Thin out the more substantial stems to near ground level to stimulate
new growth.

Bougainvillea spectabilis

Callistemon
(bottle brush)   This bush should be pruned back lightly in the autumn after
flowering.

It has only a very few dormant buds from which new growth can arise,
and therefore hard pruning is not recommended. It is sometimes
necessary to remove a few of the older branches from more mature
shrubs to encourage the growth of new shoots.

Callistemon citrinus

123

Cistus (rock rose)   This is a troublesome plant. New shoots almost never grow from old wood, and so pruning should be restricted to the removal of dead wood. Frost-bitten plants rarely recover.

Citrus (lemon, orange)   Prune back any shoots which become too long. When pruning, look for a terminal bud which is pointing in the right direction (outwards) to encourage the plant to form a good shape.

Clerodendrum   Thin out this bush in spring. Remove the oldest branches from the centre of the bush.

Clivia   This plant's flowers will be pollinated by summer insects if it is set outside in a shady spot. The result is a display of beautiful, round seeds which turn from green to red. Once the seeds have turned red, you should remove the flower stalk to conserve the plant's energy.

Cupressus (cypress)   In colder climates it will only be possible to grow cypresses on sheltered patios or in unheated greenhouses. You can pinch out the outermost terminal buds to encourage bushy growth, but cypresses will spread out well even when not pruned.

Datura (syn. Brugmansia)   In late autumn, cut back the parts which are becoming woody to leave a height of 50cm (20in).

Cistus *x* corbariensis

Citrus *plants*

Erythrina crista-galli

Erythrina (coral tree) Shoots from this bush should be pruned back to old wood in spring. This will encourage better and longer-lasting flowers on the resulting new growth.

Fatsia japonica

Fatsia Prune back extremely overgrown plants in spring. The plant will then produce healthy, new growth.

Ficus The species of *Ficus* which requires most pruning is *F. benjamina*. A plant which has grown too large should have its protruding branches removed. Always prune back down to a lateral. To keep a plant low-growing, you can always top the leader, making your cut above a lateral that is growing at a slight upwards angle. This will make your pruning almost imperceptible. Other *Ficus* species are best dealt with either by guiding their protruding shoots downwards towards the soil or by air layering. If the leader is topped, the uppermost dormant buds will produce new laterals, which will grow above the leader stem. You will have shot yourself neatly in the foot: you will not have restricted the plant's size, and its shape will have been lost for ever.

Fuchsia

Fuchsia Before bringing a potted fuchsia indoors in autumn, cut off its longer shoots. In early spring, cut them back again to just above old wood. The strong buds at the base of the branches will then begin to break.

125

Grevillea This fast growing plant should be pruned in spring. It will then start to produce new growth immediately. To prevent these plants from becoming straggly, you should place them in a well lit area. Whatever you do, they should not be allowed to become too warm. Growing them in a cool environment will mean less pruning.

Lantana *arrived in Europe at the end of the 17th century and quickly became a popular plant in orangeries.*

Hibiscus Prune back the longer stems in early spring to maintain the hibiscus' attractively bushy shape. If needs be, you can prune it back all over: it will produce healthy, new growth again if you do. Leave a few buds on the laterals to encourage the growth of new shoots. Hibiscus is often treated with growth inhibitors to keep it growing low. If you want to grow a massive hibiscus, you will have to wash the soil off its roots (which may contain growth inhibitor) and give the plant completely fresh soil. Treated this way, the plant will start growing well again after only a short period of inactivity.

Hydrangea Hydrangeas which are grown as house plants require just a very little pruning. Finished flowers can be cut off with part of the stalk just above a point where you can see strong buds.

Lantana Regular topping creates a nice branching structure. You can create a standard form with a clear leg by allowing one leader to grow, only topping it once it has reached the height of your own choosing.

| Laurus (bay laurel) | Bay can be trimmed into a sphere or pyramid using kitchen scissors. Pruning should be done in early spring and in August. Use secateurs for this. If you were to use hedging shears, you would cut a great many leaves in half. While not so terrible in itself, the plant would look very ugly indeed with all the resulting brown edges. You should give a bay tree time to produce new growth before pruning it if it has been damaged by frost. Only then should you cut off the frost-bitten sections. |

Myrtus communis

Leptospermum (Manuka or tea tree) This New Zealand shrub should not be cut back to bare wood. Doing this would greatly increase the chances of the plant being unable to produce new growth ever again. Thin out a few of the flowering branches once their display has finished.

Malvaviscus Prune this plant in the same way as for abutilon and African hemp (*Sparmannia*).

Myrtus (myrtle) This plant requires little pruning, but try to keep it in good shape. It should be pruned in autumn once it has completely finished flowering.

Nerium (oleander) Cut all of last season's wood back to its base once flowering is over in autumn. Do not prune at all if you want your oleander to grow into a much larger plant.

Laurus nobilis

127

Passiflora caerulea

Olea (olive)   If you do not prune an olive its shoots will become straggly and weak. Terminal buds should be pinched out continuously once four to six pairs of leaves have grown on any one stem. Take care to notice in which direction the remaining uppermost bud is pointing: pinch out shoots all the way back to a bud which faces in the right direction. This will put you in charge of the direction in which your plant is to grow.

Parthenocissus (Virginia creeper)   Prune Virginia creeper as you would a grape vine: leave its branching structure intact but cut back its new shoots in spring. Sometimes you will have to prune back the major stems as well if frost damage has occurred in an unheated greenhouse.

Passiflora (passion flower)   Passion flowers grow so fast that it does not much matter how you prune them. For preference, leave old wood untouched: the plant will then flower on new growth from this wood. If a passion flower has become too entangled it can always be cut down completely. The result will be that it flowers later in the season.

Pittosporum   This is an ideal plant for the conservatory or greenhouse. Have no fear of pruning this shrub, but do try to keep its shape intact. It can be stooled should frost damage occur, but will quickly produce regenerative growth.

Right: Plumbago auriculata

Plumbago	Tie in this plant's leaders and prune back its laterals. If, despite all your efforts, the plant should become frost-bitten, it can be cut back completely and, in most cases, will produce new growth again - even after this kind of severe treatment. This plant can also be trained. You can cut back its laterals to two or three buds from the leader stem.

Viburnum tinus

Rhododendron (azalea)	Long, straggly branches growing from a Japanese azalea can be pruned back to keep the bush trim. Under ideal conditions, azaleas can live to an extremely old age. Where an azalea is growing under such ideal conditions, you might even want to consider using it for (free-form) topiary.

Rhoicissus	Hard pruning is, now and then, essential for this plant. Thin out rigorously to prevent older leaves from turning brown and dying off.

Sparmannia
(African help)

Sparmannia (African hemp)	African hemp can be cut back in spring after having been dormant in a cool room. Once cut back, it can be placed outdoors about the beginning of June. If you take good care of this plant, it can reach a height of 2m (6ft) by September.

Viburnum (laurustinus)	*Viburnum tinus* (laurustinus) does not need pruning. Also, do not dead head old flowers as the plant will later provide you with a beautiful display of bunched berries.

Useful addresses

Canada   *Gardens to visit*

Jardin Botanique de Montréal
(Montreal Botanic Garden)
4101 Rue Sherbrooke Est
Montréal (Québec)
H1X 2B2

Botanic Gardens
University of British Columbia
Vancouver
British Columbia

United Kingdom   *Garden Centres and Nurseries*

The Herb Nursery
Grange Farm
Main Street
Thistleton
Rutland LE15 7RE

Naked Cross Nurseries
Waterloo Road
Corfe Mullen
Wimborne
Dorset BH21 3SR

Rumwood Nurseries Ltd
Langley
Maidstone
Kent ME17 3ND

St Bridget Nurseries Ltd
Old Rydon Lane
Exeter
Devon EX2 7JY

Stydd Nursery
Stonygate Lane
Ribchester
Nr Preston
Lancashire PR3 3YN

Allowing climbers to use an older tree as support will not cause any harm to the tree. In forests it is quite normal to find ivy (Hedera helix) climbing up tree trunks.

Thyme House Nursery
Manea March
Cambridgeshire

Weasdale Nurseries
Kirkby Stephen
Cumbria CA17 4LX

World's End Nurseries
441- 457 King's Road
London SW10

Gardens to visit

Claremont Landscape Gardens
Portsmouth Road
Esher
Surrey KT10 5JG

Gardens of England and Wales
The National Garden Scheme
Hatchlands Park
East Clandon
Surrey GU4 7RT

Seed suppliers

Chiltern Seeds
Bortree Stile
Ulverston
Cumbria LA12 7PB

D.T. Brown & Co Ltd
Station Road
Poulton-le-Fylde
Blackpool
Lancashire FY6 7HX

W. Robinson & Sons Ltd
Sunny Bank
Forton
Nr Preston
Lancashire PR3 0BN

Stewart's (Nottingham) Ltd
3 George Street
Nottingham NG1 3BH

Garden Services and
Equipment

Axminster Power Tool Centre
Chard Street
Axminster
Devon EX13 5DZ

D. Bennet Garden Services
53 Philpot Square
Peterborough Road
London SW6 3HT

Chase Organics (GB) Ltd
Coombelands House
Addlestone
Weybridge
Surrey KT15 1HY

American Horticultural Society
7931 East Boulevard Drive
Alexandria, VA 22308 -1300

United States of
America

Massachusetts Horticultural
Society
300 Massachusetts Avenue
Boston, MA 02115

Pacific Horticultural
Foundation
Box 485
Berkeley, CA 94941

Gardens to visit

Brooklyn Botanic Garden
1000 Washington Avenue
Brooklyn, NY 11225

A pruning saw or lopper mounted on a telescopic pole can be used to cut many branches while the gardener is still at ground level. The same pole can be used in summer for plucking apples. Special baskets or nets can be purchased for this purpose.

The Huntingdon Botanical Gardens
San Marino
California

The Huntingdon Library, art collections and botanical gardens, has thirteen different gardens.

Here, too, you can see just how useful a telescopic pole can be.

New York Botanical Garden
Southern Boulevard & 200th Street
Bronx, NY 10438

For more information on gardens to visit, please contact your local Cooperative Extension Agent or your State University Department of Agriculture.

Mulberries growing up a lattice frame against the author's garage.

Glossary of terms

This glossary contains simple explanations of the pruning terms used in the text. These terms are also used by tree-nurserymen, horticulturists, park department workers, botanists, and gardening historians. I have not sought to give precise definitions – these can be found in dictionaries.

A rhododendron's flower bud. On some shrubs the difference between leaf buds and flower buds can be seen as early as winter.

Adventitious bud
A bud formed by chance which starts growing spontaneously or after an injury, usually producing long, strongly growing shoots. These often appear around pruning wounds. Also known as water shoots.

Air layering
A method of producing new plants from old, leggy specimens. A cut is made towards the top of the plant, which is wrapped in damp sphagnum moss and then sealed in polythene film. Eventually, new roots will grow from the cut and the top can then be removed and planted up. This technique can be used for some species of *Ficus*.

Alternate
A term to describe plant internodes which do not grow in a straight line, as in the lime tree, for example.

Alternate fruiting
This is a fruit-tree term. Alternate fruiting means that, while one year will see a large yield in fruit, the next year will be poor. The cause of this is unknown.

Anvil-type pruning shears
Secateurs or lopper with one blade that cuts on an opposing flat surface.

Apex
The tip of a stem. The apical bud is the uppermost on a stem. The apical shoot is the highest on a branching system.

Apical bud/shoot
See Apex.

Arbour
Ornamental latticework used as a seating area or summer-house and which also serves as a support for climbers.

Arbour avenues
Trees planted at regular intervals. These are often pruned and clipped to form a screen or roof, either for

aesthetic reasons or to provide
shade.

Arbour retreat
Latticework above a seating
area, over which climbers have
been allowed to grow.

Axiliary bud
A bud which is formed in the
angle between leaf stalk and
stem.

Bark
A tree's outer layer of dead,
corky cells which are added to
each year. This often splits
owing to the tree's expanding
circumference. Bark provides a
tree with a protective layer, as
does the phloem.

Bark ringing
A means of stalling growth and
increasing production of flower
buds in fruit trees whereby a
ring, or section, of the bark and
phloem is removed from the
trunk.

Berceau
A covered walkway planted
with hedging to form a tunnel.
Openings are often made in a
berceau to create "windows."

Bleeding
Sap flowing from a wound
caused, for example, by pruning. The late pruning of old
wood in grapes and maples
leads to unstoppable
"bleeding."

Boscage
A geometrically shaped coppice
surrounded by (high) hedging.

Bow saw
A saw with a removable blade
held in place by a clamp.

Branch
A lateral, usually woody and
more than one year old.

Break shoots
Shoots which arise from a leaf
axil. Shoots usually grow out
from leaf axils after one year.

Breaking bud
A bud which is on the point of
producing growth.

Budding
The grafting technique whereby
a scion bud or shoot is inserted
in an opening in the bark of the
rootstock.
Budding unions are common
in fruit trees, roses, and
weeping forms of trees and
shrubs.

Budding height
The height on the rootstock
stem at which the scion bud has
been inserted.

Bush
A shrub which usually grows in
an undisciplined, natural way.
A bush is not necessarily woody.
Bush is the term used for
shrubby species found in
nature, while shrub is used for
cultivated plants.

Bush form
For fruit trees this describes a
tree with a short central leader
from which branches radiate,
somewhere between a (dwarf)
pyramid and a half-standard.

*Ensure that there is enough space
between the tree and its stake. The tree
collar should not be too tight.*

Buttressed wall
A training wall with alcoves.

Cabinet
An small area in a garden
bounded by high, geometrically
shaped hedges.

Callus
Corky tissue which grows over a
pruning wound or injury.

Candelabra form
A term concerning trained fruit
trees; a fan espalier in the shape
of a candelabra.

Candelabra pruning
The sawing off of laterals in
older trees; the uppermost
branches are cut shorter than
the lower ones. Candelabra
pruning is sometimes necessary
when the roots of a tree have
been seriously damaged during
transplantation.

An Austrian pine with new shoots.

Central leader
The clear main stem of a plant.

Cloaking
Shoots growing on a tree trunk to protect it from sun scorch. Beech (*Fagus*) and hornbeam (*Carpinus*) are particularly sensitive to scorching, which explains why they hold on to their dead leaves in winter.

Collar
Thick corky tissue around the crotch formed between a leader and an issuing branch.

Columnar
Trees which have a naturally columnar growth pattern, such as the Japanese cherry *Prunus serrulata* 'Amanogawa.' Trees with the species name 'Fastigiata' are all upward growing and often columnar.

Columnar tree
A natural growth pattern in

which no major laterals grow. An example of this is the apple 'Ballerina.'

Coppice/coppicing
Woodland trees which are regularly felled for local usage. These were common in the past. As a result of constant felling, coppiced trees have spindly trunks which grow from the original tree stump. This kind of forestry requires the regular felling of re-emergent trees. The practice is also known as stooling.

Cordon
A small tree restricted to one central leader stem through pruning.

Covered arch
Latticework arch over which climbers can be grown.

"Creative pruning"
The excessive pruning of evergreen shrubs just before Christmas to an extent that is beyond what is beneficial to the plant. Professional growers are sometimes guilty of this when they try to supply large quantities of cheap, seasonal greenery.

Crossed branch
A branch or lateral running right through a bush and thereby crossing and rubbing against other branches, damaging bark and phloem in the process.

Crown
The uppermost part of a tree's

stem from which the branches grow. It is also a term used to indicate the basal part of a herbaceous perennial or current growth where woody rings are starting to appear (the remains of bud scales).

Crowning up
Removal of the lowest branches from a tree's trunk to give it better standard tree proportions: one third trunk, or leg, and two thirds crown. Also known as "pruning up." Crowning up too high is known as "mistreatment."

Cultivar (an abbreviation of "cultivated variety")
A plant which has been propagated or created by means of cultivation.
Where a cross or hybrid occurs in nature, this is called a "variety."
A cultivar's name is always written with a capital letter and placed within inverted commas to show that it differs from natural varieties.

Current growth
This describes the stems or shoots produced in the current season from which flowers are produced that same year. (As a rule, this describes late-flowering shrubs.)

Cylinder form
A cylindrically trained form on a short central leader.

Dormant bud
An undeveloped bud or node which will develop if the buds

above it should fail to break. For example, if they have been pruned out.

Espalier
Trees and shrubs where opposing branches have been trained horizontally at intervals into tiers.

Eye
An undeveloped growth bud. Bud is the term most frequently used for woody plants, while eye is usually used for grape vines.

Fan-trained
A trained tree where the branches form a fan shape.

Feathered trees
A young tree with laterals, two or three years old. Feathered trees were once exclusively seedlings, but nowadays they are also produced from cuttings. The

An old, trained lime at Domies Toen in Pieterburen.

term is often used in forestry and tree nurseries.

Flower bud
Unlike leaf buds and wood (growth) buds, these buds only produce flowers.

Flush cut
A stem which is cut away with a pruning knife so closely to its place of origin that any dormant buds there are also removed.

Fruiting spur
A branch bearing a cluster of flower buds, particularly on fruit trees. These do not necessarily grow vertically: such branches can also grow horizontally or at an angle.

Grafting
Uniting a stem or bud from one plant with the rootstock of another to create a new plant.

Grecian saw
See Pruning saw.

Growth buds
Also known as growth tips. These buds extend the branching system.

Growth shoots
A shoot which has reached a length of more than 50cm (20in) and which produces little in the way of flowers and fruits.

Half-standard
A tree form where the trunk or stem is short. Minimum height is 1.1-1.2m (31/2-4ft).

A tree being subjected to candelabra pruning. Only turn to this drastic pruning technique in emergencies.

Hand shears
A smaller version of hedging shears, suitable for clipping box.

Hard pruning
Also referred to as severe pruning. This involves pruning laterals a long way back.

Hedge
A partition formed by trees or bushes which have been planted at regular intervals from one other.

Hedging shears
Large or small shears for clipping hedges (*see* Hand shears).

Herbaceous plants
Any plant lacking a woody stem which dies back in winter.

A row of crowned-up trees. The right proportions should be maintained when crowning up a tree: two thirds crown and one third trunk (or leg)..

Incompatibility
Incompatibility describes the inability of a scion and rootstock to form a union. See Mid-section scions.

Internode
The length of stem between nodes or buds, or between two leaves if these have already grown.

Last season's wood
A stem or branch which grew in the previous year and from which flowers are produced the following year. Early-flowering shrubs almost all flower on last season's wood.

Lateral
A stem or shoot branching off from a larger one at a leaf axil. Sublaterals are further growths from laterals.

Lawn clippers
Garden shears of the same type as those used for the manual shearing of sheep.

Layer
A branch or stem lying along the ground where it produces roots. These can be pruned off and used as new plants.

Leader
The main stem, or the branches of a tree or shrub which extend the existing branch system.

Leader bud
The final growth bud at the end of leader branches and shoots. Also known as growth tips or terminal buds.

Leaf bud
Only leaves arise from these buds, unlike flower buds and wood (growth) buds.

Leaf scar
A permanent scar left after the leaf has fallen.

Leg
A leg is the main stem, or leader, of a tree or shrub which has been shorn of laterals to a particular length to produce a clean trunk.

Light pruning
Little is pruned from the plant (leaving long laterals).

Long-handled lopper
A pruning tool, essentially secateurs but with long handles which reach a greater distance and provide greater pruning strength.

Maiden
A young tree or bush in its first year. Its laterals are known as feathers.

Marking
Removal of the bark at eye-level on selected tree trunks to indicate which ones are to be cut down. (This kind of marking is used in forestry, public parks and gardens, and for trees planted along roadsides.)

Marking knife
A special tool for marking.

Mid-section scions
Mid-section scions are particularly common in pear trees. A mid-section scion is used if there is incompatibility between the rootstock and the cultivated form to be grown from a scion.
Two grafting points are visible on such trees.

Mixed spur
A spur or short shoot with a mixture of wood buds and flower buds.

Morbid growth
Rapid growth which ensues after over-severe pruning has disturbed the balance between roots and branches.

Mulch layer
A layer of organic material given to a plant as fertilizer and to prevent the upper soil layer from drying out.

Mutants
Aberrant flowers or shoots which arise spontaneously. These are often seen in plants with variegated leaves and double flowers: leaves suddenly appear that are entirely green or flowers are borne singly. Also known as sports or chimaeras.

Notching
A cut into the bark and phloem above a bud in order to stimulate that bud's growth.

Old wood
Flowers produced on old wood develop on stems formed in the previous year or the year before that.

Open-centre bush form
Also known as the forked or Y-form.
A trained tree or shrub with two strong leaders of more or less equal size which form an angle of approximately ninety degrees with each other.

Outward bud
A bud facing outwards; also known as an outer eye.

Palmette
A palm-shaped espalier.

Palm's length
A palm's length is 10cm (4in).

Pergola
Foliage-covered walkway made from wooden poles and beams as supports for climbing plants.

Phloem
A layer of cells below the bark which serves as protection. The phloem conveys foodstuffs from the leaves to a plant's roots.

Pleaching
Training trees, usually lime and hornbeam, to grow into each other to form screens or arches.

Pole pruner
Pruning shears attached to a pole and operated by means of a wire running along its length.

Pollarding
Regular pruning of shoots and branches right back to the trunk. The most familiar example is that of pollarded willows.

Pruning knife
A generally curved knife for taking cuttings and for pruning.

Pruning saw
A saw for pruning tree branches. These come in all sizes and lengths of handle. Some

*A shaped, columnar oak (*Quercus robur *'Fastigiata').*

have curved blades. The biggest, for large branches, is called a Grecian saw.

Pruning up
See Crowning up.

Pyramid form
Concerning pears: a cone shape in which laterals are arranged in tiers, the lower laterals being longer than those higher up.

Remontant
Repeat flowering. Unlike roses which flower once or perpetually during the growing season, remontant roses (or hybrid perpetuals) flower at intervals throughout the season.

Renewal pruning
Also known as rejuvenation pruning. Renewal pruning entails the gradual removal of older laterals so that new ones can grow back in their place.

Root pruning

Root pruning may need to be done during transplantation if roots are too big for the hole dug for the plant. Root pruning is also carried out to slow down growth in certain fruit trees which otherwise grow too vigorously. The larger roots surrounding the tree are cut through.

Rootstock

The lowest part of a tree or shrub and on to which cultivated scions are grafted or budded.

Rubbing out

Removal of shoots growing from the leaf axil, especially in tomatoes. Also the removal of lateral buds to allow the apical bud to grow more strongly. This is a technique commonly employed by flower growers, particularly for dahlias, chrysanthemums, and carnations.

Scion

A shoot or bud removed from a plant for budding or grafting on rootstock.

Secateurs

Pruning shears, or scissors, available in left-handed versions as well as for right-handed users. There is often a hollow in the blade close to the pivot for cutting (thin) wire.

Seedling

Unlike plants from cuttings or grafting, a seedling is a plant which has been grown from seed.

Shaped tree

A tree which has been clipped into a particular shape (topiary). Trained fruit trees can also be shaped.

Shoot

A sappy growth which has not yet become woody and is usually still green, or any recent growth.

Shrub

Woody plant where the branches or stems grow either from the ground or from a point low down on a central leader.
- 1st order shrubs grow taller than 4m (13ft).
- 2nd order shrubs grow to a height of between 2 and 4m (6 and 13ft).
- 3rd order shrubs grow to a height of between 50cm and 2m (20in and 6ft).
- 4th order shrubs grow to a height of up to 50cm (20in).

Species

An individual plant which occurs in nature within a genus of related plants. Defined by the second word of its scientific name.

Spur

A short shoot from which flowers are produced, usually the following season. (*See* Fruiting spur.)

Standard

A tree with a clear leg or trunk at least 1.8m (5ft10in) in height.

Stock

See Rootstock.

Stool

A tree or shrub growing as a clump of stems or leaders from ground level.
Three birches planted closely together do not constitute a beech stool. A true stool is produced from one tree. See Stooling.

Stooling

The practice of cutting down shrubs and trees to ground level to maintain a clump of young stems.

Stopping

Breaking off or pinching out the apex of a plant or the end of sappy shoots with the fingers.

Stopping leader buds

A keen-edged pruning knife is used to remove the outermost growth tips of leaders in conifers and fruit trees to encourage the growth of more laterals.

Stub

The section of a branch which remains after bad pruning. Stubs often fail to heal or grow over, which results in bacterial and fungal infections entering the tree or shrub.

Suckers

This refers to shoots growing from rootstock, usually appearing from the roots. Many plants are grafted in order to improve flowering, growth, fruit yields, or (in the case of roses) to counter the production of suckers from rootstock.

Summer pruning
A pruning session which takes place during the growing season or once terminal or apical buds have been formed (in August). Summer pruning of fruit trees has a beneficial effect on the blossom they subsequently produce.

Switch
Cut willow twigs which have various uses, including basket weaving.

Telescopic pole
An extendible construction on which a saw, secateurs, or pole pruner can be mounted.

Terminal bud
This describes the bud at the tip of a leader or shoot. *See* Apex.

Thinning out
When this term concerns young plantation trees, thinning out means that a percentage of the trees is completely removed to give the others more room to grow. In terms of pruning it means removing a number of branches or stems from a bush to give it more light and air.

Tool belt
A leather bag in which pruning tools are kept and which can be attached to a belt.

Topiary
The art of shaping trees and bushes into artificial designs: geometric shapes such as spheres, cubes, pyramids, and spirals, or other designs including animals.

Clipped columns of larch.

Yew and box are typically used for this.

Topping
This involves removing the uppermost part of a plant's central leader to restrict upward growth and thus strengthen the branching system. Topping is often the result of bad pruning.

Trained trees or shrubs
A tree or shrub which is grown in a two-dimensional shape up against a wall or else free-standing against lattice or wires.

Training wall
A wall against which fruit trees, for example, are trained.

Tree
A woody plant with a clearly defined stem from which branches arise at a height of 2m (6ft) at maturity:
- 1st order trees grow taller than 15m (50ft).
- 2nd order trees grow to a height of between 10 and 15m (35 and 50ft).
- 3rd order trees grow to a height of between 6 and 10m (20 and 35ft).

Tree collar
A reinforced rubber ring which is secured around young trees and attached to a stake.

Tree radius
A bare, circular area under a tree which measures the radius of the tree's crown. This radius is less than that of the crown when beneath fruit trees.

Trellis
Latticework which is both decorative and a support for climbing plants.

Twig
A shoot of one year old which has become woody.

Union
The point at which the scion of a cultivated plant is grafted on

rootstock. The union is often visible on roses and fruit trees; in other plants it is less easy to make out.

Variety

A variation on a species which has arisen naturally. *See* Cultivar.

Water shoots

See Adventitious buds.

Weeping form

Trees or shrubs with drooping branches. The scientific name used to describe such species is usually *pendula*, such as *Betula pendula* (weeping birch), for example. In cultivated varieties, this classification is shown with a capital letter between inverted commas: *Fagus sylvatica* 'Pendula.'

Whip

Older than a maiden, and with an erect, main stem from which all laterals have been removed to leave only a covering of small side-growths. This is because the plant is not yet mature enough for crowning up into a standard tree shape.

Winter pruning

A pruning session which takes place while the tree or shrub is dormant, in other words from December to March.

Woody plants

Plants with woody stems as opposed to herbaceous plants.

Left: Hardy fuchsias bloom on current growth and so can be cut back to ground level in spring. This is Fuchsia magellanica 'Alba.'

Topiary is displayed at its best in winter.

Picture credits

G. Otter, IJsselstein: cover, pages 4, 6 bottom, 13, 14, 15, 16, 18, 19 bottom, 20, 21, 22, 23, 28, 29, 35 top, 44, 49, 60, 63, 64, 68 bottom, 83 right, 90, 91 bottom, 98, 100 right, 101, 102, 103, 104 left, 106-107, 108, 109 left, 111 right, 113 bottom right, 114 bottom left, 116, 120 left, 122 top, 124, 125 bottom, 126, 127, 128, 130 top, 132, 133 bottom.

J.A. van Lienden-Geenen, Eelde: pages 7 top, 17, 34, 38 left, 39, 42, 91 top, 95 left, 96, 114 top left, 134, 137 top, 138.

Klaas T. Noordhuis, Leens: pages 6 top, 7 bottom, 10, 11, 12, 19 top, 24, 25, 27, 30, 31, 32, 33, 35 bottom, 36 left, 38 right, 40-41, 43, 46, 47, 48, 50, 51, 52, 53, 54, 55, 57, 61, 62, 65, 66, 67 top, 68 top, 69, 70 right, 71, 75 bottom, 76, 78, 80, 81, 82, 83 left, 84 top, 86 bottom, 88, 89, 92, 93, 94, 95 right, 97, 99, 100 left, 104 right, 105, 109 bottom right, 110, 111 left, 113 left and top right, 114 right, 115, 117, 119, 120 right, 121, 131, 133 top, 135, 136, 139, 141, 142, 143.

H. Reitsema, Den Andel: pages 9, 26, 36 right, 37, 45, 59, 67 bottom, 70 left, 72, 73, 74 right, 75 top, 77, 79, 84 bottom, 85, 86 top, 87, 109 top right, 112, 118, 123 bottom, 137 bottom.

P. Schut, Amsterdam: pages 8, 74 left.

N. Vermeulen, Groningen: pages 122 bottom, 123 top, 125 top, 129, 130 bottom.